Preparing Your Child
To Love God

Preparing Your Child To Love God

Anna B. Mow

Zondervan Publishing House
Grand Rapids, Michigan

PREPARING YOUR CHILD TO LOVE GOD
Copyright © 1983 by The Zondervan Corporation
Grand Rapids, Michigan

This book was formerly published under the title
Your Child—From Birth to Rebirth
Copyright © 1963 by Zondervan Publishing House

Library of Congress Cataloging in Publication Data

Mow, Anna B.
  Preparing your child to love God.

  Previously published as: Your child—from birth to rebirth. c1963.
  Bibliography: p.
  1. Christian education of children.   2. Children—
Religious life.   I. Title.
BV1475.2.M6   1983   207   83-21917
ISBN 0-310-29631-5

Printed in the United States of America

83   84   85   86   87   88 — 10   9   8   7   6   5   4   3   2   1

Dedicated to
Concerned Parents
and
Teachers of Children

Preface

A friend wrote, "Michael, my six-year-old, had just gone to bed, and as usual he had to relate the day's happenings. This particular day he had been playing with five-year-old Timmy. He said, 'Mama, sometimes I just don't understand Timmy and sometimes he can't understand me.' I asked him why. 'Well,' he replied, 'today I tried to tell him about Jesus being crucified and he just couldn't understand me, but he asked me, "Why did God make a bad man like Satan?" I told him that God didn't make him a bad man, because He made him a *good* angel. Satan made himself bad, because he wanted to be bigger than God. So God had to put him out of heaven because nobody can be bigger than God.' "

Tell such a story to a group of religious educators and listen to the inevitable argument that would follow about a six-year-old's understanding or even his exposure to such talk.

Then suppose Jesus walked into the room in the midst of the discussion: so warm and alert always toward any response from a child. Perhaps He would say, "See that you underestimate none of these little ones, for I tell you, that their angels in heaven are forever looking at the face of My heavenly Father" (see Matt. 18:10).

Real learning comes in stages. Someone asked a little girl what she had learned on her first day in school. She replied, "I learned things I did not understand and then I learned to understand them." Most of our learning about God is like that at any age. We think we know something, then later a new awareness or illumination comes and we feel that we knew nothing but the words before. As I grew up I read many love stories, but when I really fell in love, it was as though I had never heard of love before. So it is in the greatest love story of all. We grow from words to deeper and deeper meanings of God's wonderful truths. Even then we cannot fully fathom the greatness of His love to us.

The church was slow through the centuries in understanding the learning capability of a child. It was a great advancement in educational insight to have graded Sunday school lessons. However, some have gone too far in withholding "content" material while others have used theological language indiscriminately. The specific use of adult religious terms does not matter as much as the failure to see what is happening in the heart and mind of the child. When he can repeat a set of words he may have nothing but the words. But even these words may be the vessel to contain real meanings later. He may also be responding to the love of the teacher instead of the words she uses. She may think he is understanding the words when he only understands her and her love. There is nothing wrong in this but we need to see that although he can readily understand the love, the understanding of the words is a *growing experience.*

A real religious understanding, besides a loving relationship and a content knowledge, requires an *illumination* that the teacher cannot give. The role of parents and teachers is to help in the preparation for this *experience that God gives.* When this awareness or illumination comes to a child he may not always realize that it is a *confrontation,* a meeting with the Lord, but he will never be able to deny the reality of such an experience. It will somehow become a point of comparison for all other experiences, whether he is conscious of this or not.

This *confrontation* should be an *expected experience.* It is more than "being good," it is more than "joining the church." It is a meeting with God as He is revealed in Jesus Christ. The daily conversation in the early church was of a *living Lord.* It was easier therefore later to come into a personal consciousness of His living presence through the Holy Spirit. In this meeting, if Christ is accepted by the young person, a *new birth* takes place. Just as the child became a member of his earthly family, he is now reborn into the *family of God.* This new relationship is more important than any other relationship in his entire life.

I want to emphasize here only the fact of an expected meeting and an acceptance of the living Lord. I do not feel it necessary now to make distinctions between being born again and the coming of the Spirit to the individual person. The disciples followed Jesus a number of years before they were filled with the Holy Spirit. There were historical reasons, if no other, for this sequence because Jesus was still with them. "By this he meant the Spirit, whom those who believed in him were later to receive. Up to that time the Spirit had not been given, since Jesus had not yet been glorified'' (John 7:39). Saul was filled with the Spirit shortly after he responded to the Damascus road vision of the Lord. Ananias came to him and said, "Brother Saul, the Lord . . . sent me so that you may see again and be filled with the Holy Spirit'' (Acts 9:17). Cornelius and those with him were filled with the Spirit *before* they were baptized (Acts 10). What happens at the beginning, or later, is by His grace and is His gift anyway. The when and how are His. Ours is to be ready for His coming into our lives. This book concerns itself primarily with that preparation.

Religious education has often been satisfied with a goal of "good character'' and has been dismayed when the goodness of the character proved to be only superficial. The purpose of *Christian* education is the *preparation of children for what God can do for and with them.* The importance of this preparation cannot be exaggerated.

The apostle Paul pictures the same truth when he says we are temples: "Don't you know that you yourselves are God's temple and that God's Spirit lives in you? If anyone destroys God's temple, God will destroy him; for God's temple is sacred, and you are that temple'' (1 Cor. 3:16, 17).

True Christian education is the preparation of this temple to make it ready for the coming in of Christ. The preparation is human responsibility. The opening of the door to Him is human responsibility. The coming in, the dwelling there, the blessings of His presence are all *gifts of His grace.* This book is about that preparation so that He may be welcome and at home in this temple.

God comes to anyone, anywhere, at any age, wherever a door is open for His coming. He does not ask us to fill out a questionnaire about our theological background or lack of it. He lets us come just as we are, with our confessions of sin and self-centeredness. All He asks is that we come with a whole heart ready to learn from Him. God is, indeed, no respecter of persons.

But what about His children who think they know the truth? It is so easy for us to pass judgment on one another. I must face the fact that there are many people with whom I disagree on many points who have learned many truths I have not yet comprehended. I want to know anything anyone has learned from the great Teacher. We each have to grow, and if we accept Him and His love toward all people we can grow by sharing with one another. You will find in the bibliography some books recommended for help that may have differing viewpoints from yours or from mine. But anyone who knows the Lord should not be afraid to listen to whatever anyone else has learned. We have our own golden rule with which to judge truth and we must use it. As one of my greatest Bible teachers used to say, "Eat the meat and throw the bones away."

The New International Version of the Bible has been used unless otherwise stated.

ANNA B. MOW

Roanoke, Virginia

Contents

Preface... 7

Part 1. You and the Children

1. Your Part in a Child's Response........................ 15
2. Your Child in the Home.............................. 23
3. Your Child in the Church............................ 33
4. The Christian Educator's Dilemma.................... 41
5. Let the Children Come............................... 51

Part 2. Preparation for Rebirth

6. Love for Relationship............................... 61
7. Imagination for Faith............................... 69
8. Choice for Commitment.............................. 79
9. Discipline for Responsibility of Choice.............. 89
10. Disciplined Mind for Discernment of Truth............ 97
11. Reverence for Worship.............................. 107
12. The Goal of the Preparation: Christian Character........ 115
13. The Secret of Character Development................. 123

Part 3. The Gift of Life

14. The Rebirth....................................... 137
15. Responsibility of Grownups in God's Family........... 145
    Bibliography...................................... 153

Part I

You and
the Children

Whoever welcomes one of these little children
in my name welcomes me.
Mark 9:37

Chapter 1

Your Part in a Child's Response

Every child comes into the world bringing with him a new chance for a better world, *provided* his parents and other adults can be awakened to their responsibility. India's great poet Tagore said: "Every child comes with the message that God is not yet discouraged of man." Each child who comes into the world presents a new possibility for lifting the destiny of the human race. A child is equipped by God for *response*. The nature of a child's response—the direction it takes—is, however, governed by the conscious or unconscious influence of some adult who is important in the child's everyday life.

Children, in a sense, hold the fate of our world in their sometimes grubby and meddlesome little hands, and if we are using our God-given intelligence we will shoulder our responsibility to them, which means much more than controlling them by whatever means in order to keep them quiet or out of the way so as to protect our own nervous systems. Shouldering our responsibility to children means we begin to understand *our part* in the development of their response mechanisms and understanding, dedicate ourselves to careful, loving, patient nurturing of those all-important responses.

How do we nurture the sensitive mechanisms of a child's response? There is only one way to begin, and that is with ourselves. We, as parents and teachers, must clarify our own concepts of God's action in a human life and we must allow His love to operate through us to them. We misrepresent our heavenly Father to our children when we lose faith in the power of His love that He revealed through Jesus, or when we hold in our own hearts a distorted view of this love. When we turn unwittingly to the methods of the world in forcing our own limited ways and thoughts on the children, are we afraid that love won't work? Or is it that we don't know about love? God's love is tender beyond measure, but never soft. It is stern, but never hard. It sees every person as a whole. Every incident is understood by Him in relation to past experience and its concomitant limitations, as well as to all possibilities for the future. This kind of love, God's kind of love, develops and keeps open the natural response of a child to others, to life itself, and prepares him for his own life response to God.

When we let ourselves be irritated by children, this irritation reveals more about ourselves than about the child. Such irritations come because of love failure within ourselves and not from without by some act of the child, however disobedient he may seem. It is this lack of God-love in ourselves that closes doors in the lives of others—not only to us, but to life and to God Himself. His kind of love *draws:* "I, if I be lifted up . . . will *draw* . . ." Jesus said. God-love draws, it never browbeats. Jesus had faith in God-love. He did not force Himself on anyone, but they were drawn to Him, then and now.

The whole biblical story of God and man centers around this astounding news that God reaches out to man even before man turns to Him. Through the centuries since the first man and woman chose to turn from God's love and fellowship, men had remained blind and stubborn in their resistance so that God had to do still more to capture their attention and secure their response. The time came for Isaiah's prophecy to be fulfilled. God sent His Son as a baby. "The virgin will be with child and will give birth to a son and they will call him 'Immanuel'— which means, 'God with us' " (Matt. 1:23). God was reaching toward man through the child, His Son, Jesus Christ. This was His supreme revelation of His unlimited love for man. God reaches first, but He gave man the responsibility of choice, therefore *He waits on man's response to Him.* God still waits for each human heart to comprehend His outreaching love and to choose to come to Him.

God has equipped every child with a natural response to love. This is the most precious quality in his life. It must be treasured so that it may grow in capacity for the day when, with all his heart, he begins to respond to the Lord of life. The fullness of God's coming to him depends on his capacity to respond to God. As Jesus grew, this response to God's love was the most natural part of His life. As He entered His ministry He always watched for response to the steadily offered love of God. His disciples were slow to learn it, but the *children* He met responded at once! Although the children of that day had been taught to stay in the background in the presence of adults, when they met Jesus all barriers were broken down. They flocked to Him naturally, gladly. How they must have delighted His heart! Their naturalness in response helped Him get His own yearning across to the grownups: "Unless you . . . become like little children, you will never enter the kingdom of heaven" (Matt. 18:3).

This natural kind of responsiveness that Jesus looked for is an outreach to life, a spontaneous and unaffected acceptance of love that purges self-centeredness and makes true self-fulfillment possible. This is the *life abundant* that Jesus came to bring and to reveal in His own life. Only such an outreach to life and to love can open the door to God's offered love. No wonder the children were such a joy to Jesus!

Apparently many Palestinian mothers understood something of how He felt toward children. "People were bringing little children to Jesus to have him touch them. . . . And he took the children in his arms, put his hands on them and blessed them." His disciples, of course, acting like most self-important adults, tried to keep the children from "bothering" Jesus. "When Jesus saw this, he was indignant. He said to them, 'Let the little children come to me, and do not hinder them, for the kingdom of God belongs to such as these. I tell you the truth, anyone who will not receive the kingdom of God like a little child will never enter it' " (Mark 10:13–16).

Feeling their adult superiority, His disciples tried to do what so many parents and teachers do: they consciously or unconsciously blocked the natural response of the children to God! Jesus was there in person to stop them, and He is here in His personal Spirit to stop today's adults from doing the same things. Our part as Christian parents and teachers is to remain sensitive to His Spirit, who lives within us. He is with us today, to guide us and to control our impatience, just as surely as He was with His disciples then. His interest in the nurturing of a child's responsiveness to Him is as keen as it was the day He set a child in the center of the circle of competitive disciples and said, "Whoever welcomes one of these little children in my name welcomes me" (Mark 9:37). He is just as keenly interested in our *understanding* the children as He was in opening the eyes of His disciples to their worth. His interest goes, according to what He had to say to them that day, beyond mere understanding of children themselves. He seemed intent upon getting across to them that when they received a child in His name they received Him too!

Could it be that as adults we have missed Him often because we have not loved and understood the children whom He loves so much? He is, of course, telling us also that there are characteristics of childhood that adults must never lose if they want to enter the kingdom of God. If the child has what it takes to be truly responsive to God, then we must understand the child better—for the sake of our own spiritual growth, as well as for increasing our ability to nurture the child's responsiveness.

A child does not enter the world with a full-grown capacity to respond. He begins life with an automatic outreach for food, for physical comfort, and an unconscious need for loving care. The uninitiated may think that the loving chatter of a mother to her newborn babe is foolish. What they do not perceive is that her loving flow of words and her constant attention are *moving him into awareness and response*. Of course, grandparents are good at this kind of talk also! Recently I spent a week in the home of new grandparents. The new grandfather, so dignified in his pulpit, was the star performer with five-week-old Debbie. He had an endless flow of chatter all ready-made for her. Her first smile in response and a week later her first ''coo'' were experiences similar to welcoming a new convert coming down the church aisle.

A baby's first smile is indeed a big event in his life—bigger than he knows! It means his capacity to respond is developing properly. The mother is smiling the child into smiling back. When the infant responds to love, he is learning the first lesson in responding to God, for God is love. Love alone has this drawing power—to bring life development out of another in the best way possible. ''We love because he first loved us'' (1 John 4:19). The child loves his mother because the mother first loved her child; loved him into response. In Jesus' time, the children, trained to draw back from unfamiliar adults, were drawn *to* Him! His understanding love did it. Only adults with this same kind of love for children can find the same response from them.

Most persons will say, and believe they are being truthful: ''Oh, I love children!'' But when? All the time? Only when they smile? With what kind of love? It is easy to love babies. They steal the show every time, as well as all available adult hearts. The test of the quality and constancy of an adult's love for a child comes when the child is less "adorable." Any child, no matter how obedient, disrupts an adult's program. Any normal child is capable of disturbing an adult's well-earned rest. His natural curiosity about life and things in general can attack an adult's nervous system and set it twanging—*unless* that adult is mature enough to recognize what is happening in the child as he reaches out to life and knowledge. The thoughtless adult thinks only about himself and his well-laid plans, and so he does not see the damage he does to a child's outreach. He should be guiding the child, but instead he has dampened the child's spirit so that the child will withdraw into himself, or he will rebel loudly against what has been done to him.

It is this preoccupation with our own affairs that blinds us to the important unfolding of a child's personality. Jesus was never preoccupied with His own affairs, even on the cross. His thought was always for others. We all remember the people who treated us with respect when we were children. My dear friend, Genie Price, is still grateful to her wise mother who, she says, never scolded or corrected her severely in public. Such incidents were between them alone and in public Genie and her mother stood together. This gives any child a sense of deeper relationship and personal dignity.

Children want to be part of the fellowship, even with adults. They want to be persons, not things to be discussed like new furniture. It can be just as damaging to "explain" a child in his hearing as to punish him before other people. It cannot be said too often that talking about a child in his presence makes him a *thing* and not a person. He wants to be a person in his own right. Children light up with new outreaching life when treated as persons, but they soak up thoughtless comments, abuse, and unkindness like a sponge, and doors to life close in on them.

I visited in a home where the youngest child, a five-year-old, was extremely shy. I attempted a conversation with the little fellow to help him forget himself. But whenever I asked him a question his parents or his sister answered for him before he could even form a sentence. They always added, by way of explanation, "Oh, he's very shy; he won't talk to strangers." (How did they know? They never gave him a chance!) He seemed to understand what I was trying to do, for after awhile he brought out some of his drawings, which were nicely done for his age. They were precious to him, an expression of his very own. His mother called them ''scribbles'' in his presence. I said, ''But this is the way a child draws.'' For the first time he really looked at me and twinkled. That night, after the service at which I spoke, he ran up the aisle to be the first to shake my hand. This was the most welcome handshake I had that night. It held in it the promise of a child's real response.

This little boy was shy and his response capacity was waiting to develop, but his ability to respond was being dwarfed daily by his well-meaning family who deprived him of nothing but the chance to grow in his own way. Children are not deaf, especially the shy ones. They are alert and as sensitive to good growing atmosphere as to a frustrating environment. It is never safe to say, ''Oh, go ahead and be careless, he won't know the difference!'' He may not analyze the difference, but he is taking it all in, to his permanent benefit or harm.

One of the most damaging of careless adult habits is to laugh *at* a child in his presence. One day I visited in the home of a lovely young couple. Their four-year-old girl was undergoing treatment for defective vision. Because of the treatment, her range of vision was constantly changing. On a given day her little chair seemed near but it was far away; the next day she would fall over it because it was closer than she thought. The child was deeply frustrated and nervous because she couldn't gauge where anything was. Just before I came in a neighbor had called. While she was there the little girl missed her chair and sat down on the floor instead. The neighbor laughed heartily, thinking it to be a good joke. But to the child it was no joke, it was a dreadful experience. She struck back at the neighbor and when I came in she did the same to me, expecting the same treatment from all adults. I knew something had happened to the child. (Her mother explained it to me the next day.) It is a crime against life to laugh *at* a child. One may laugh only *with* a child.

We block a child's outreach to life unwittingly and often because we are not conscious of what is happening to and in the child. I had never realized how frequently I failed my children until the day I saw a startling contrast between two teachers. It was visiting day at our children's school. The pupils in the first room I visited were having a drill in decimals. No one seemed to know any answers. The nervous teacher was frustrated and embarrassed, painfully aware of the row of mothers in the back of the room. This made the children self-conscious too. To each bewildered child she would snap, ''What's the matter with you today? You knew it yesterday!'' Her despair and frustration made the atmosphere so uncomfortable that no mother stayed long. The children had to stay, perplexed by their own failure and by their teacher's impatience. They were all the more bewildered because she was usually so patient.

In the next room I visited, the children were reviewing their multiplication tables. The relaxed, smiling teacher paid no attention whatever to the visiting mothers. She wasn't in a hurry; she took plenty of time to wait for each child's answer. I shall never forget one shy little girl. ''How much is five times seven?'' the teacher asked her. She could not answer. Hands went up all over the room, but the teacher said, ''All of you put your hands down. Dorothy knows the answer. I know she does. We'll wait for her.'' Then she looked at the little girl so sweetly and so patiently that she seemed to surround the child with love to the exclusion of the whole room. Nothing was more important right then than that one shy little girl should find her courage. When the answer came, the teacher rejoiced: ''I knew you could do it!'' That was a lesson in life more than in arithmetic.

It is a great gift to a child to build up his courage so that he can walk always in hope and faith, no matter what happens to him. Those who break a child's spirit must answer to Jesus Christ. After all, He said plainly: ''Whoever welcomes a little child like this in my name welcomes me. But if anyone causes one of these little ones who believe in me to sin, it would be better for him to have a huge millstone hung around his neck and to be drowned in the depths of the sea'' (Matt. 18:5,6).

Strong words, these, but the Son of God said them—not to pile guilt on us for what damage we have already done to our children—He said them to clear up for us once and for all, the sobering *fact* of our responsibility to any child under our care. If we make it clear at the outset that we adults govern the actual growth of a child's capacity to respond, we will daily be clearing the way for him as he moves toward the all-important day when he will be *able* to respond by his own maturing choice in his personal commitment for life to the Lord Himself.

The condition of the child's responsiveness during the vital years from *birth to rebirth* is in the hands of the adults who people his world. Every minute of every hour of every day counts in a child's life, until he is old enough to put his own will into receiving the Lord of Life—and then in the years beyond, as he grows in his own knowledge of this Lord who loves him—and all of us more than we can ever comprehend.

Homework for Parents—

- For one week keep a record of your relationship with your child.
- Note every time your child opens up and reaches out to you.
- Note any time you close doors in your child's life.
- Find out why he closed up. Was it your fault?
- Or is he unable to cope with untoward circumstances?
- Watch his interest in life around him. Guard and direct every outreach of his life in order to keep him open to life.

Chapter 2
Your Child in the Home

Real religion is a matter of our life relationships much more than it is a matter of words. We start too late if we begin our teaching about God with *words*. Too many Christians have thought of God in verbal terms only. They are seemingly satisfied with the things that can be said *about* Him. Words are important and have their rightful place but another foundation must come first. *This foundation is built in the relationship of the home.* If the church must bear the brunt of the verbal teaching without this foundation experience in the home it is as if the foundation were built on top of the walls instead of under them.

The late Dr. C. C. Ellis of Juniata College wondered one day why some of the devout Christian leaders of the last century should have objected to the Sunday school movement. Why did they object to the church teaching religion to the children? Alert scholar that he was, he went to the archives of old Eastern Pennsylvania churches to find what reasons they gave in their council meeting minutes for such objections. To his astonishment it was not that they were reluctant to take on something new. Instead he found their recorded objection to be: If the church takes up the teaching of the children, the homes will let it go and will leave the responsibility to the church. How discerning the old brethren were! That is exactly what has happened. Many children know only what they learn at church about the Bible, about prayer, about religion. Too many homes are secular places for eating and sleeping and watching television, even though the parents may be churchgoers. But the foundation for religious teaching must be in the home.

When it comes to life values, the teaching without words must precede the use of words, or the words will never be fully understood. The life before words are understood begins in the home in the life of the little child. Before he can understand words he learns many important things that help build the foundation for his life. These are unconscious learnings, but they are basic, nevertheless.

This basic unconscious learning is even more pertinent in the things of God. But through the ages the man of religion has lost himself in the words of his *faith* and has lost the *life* the words were intended to communicate. God had mercy, so "the Word became flesh and lived for a while among us" (John 1:14), so that men could truly see what God was trying to communicate. Even when the Son of God lived among men, religious leaders were so lost in the *words of religion* that they could not see the *Word of God*. In their blindness and religious arrogance they crucified the Revealer. But the revelation remains, for He had lived *the truth*. After knowing the Word we may use the words He gave us.

Even before the revelation in Jesus the early Israelites recognized these great teaching truths:

> Hear, O Israel: The Lord our God, the Lord is one. Love the Lord your God with all your heart and with all your soul and with all your strength. These commandments that I give you today are to be upon your hearts. Impress them on your children. Talk about them when you sit at home and when you walk along the road, when you lie down and when you get up. Tie them as symbols on your hands and bind them on your foreheads. Write them on the door-frames of your houses and on your gates.
>
> (Deut. 6:4–9).

The Israelites first expected the *parents to be whole in their own response to God* (vv. 4,5). This is the basic teaching method, the greatest method of all—the *living* of the truth. Even then they saw that this was the basic learning method of every child. There is no substitute for the *unconscious teaching* that communicates *what we are* long before any teaching can be communicated by words. When the child finally learns the words he will be able to say, "Oh, yes, I knew that long ago."

Then those wise people of ancient times saw the importance of the *informal teaching* parents were doing every day (vv. 6,7). This method also outweighs and undergirds all formal teaching. This is learning for all of life, not just during special hours: when sitting at home, while going for a walk, when going to bed, and when getting up in the morning. What lovely home scenes this pictures for us! The family sitting in the home at dusk talking about God's love for each one; Father taking the children for a walk telling about the lovely things God has created; Mother lying down for a moment in loving fellowship with the child after evening prayer; the cheery call in the morning: Time to get up. "This is the day the LORD has made; let us rejoice and be glad in it" (Ps. 118:24). In other words, the parents should talk about God as naturally as they talk about food and clothes. This suits the understanding of a child because to him there is no distinction between the secular and the sacred. In this the child is more Christlike than adults are, for God belongs in all of life.

The third method emphasized for religious education in the home in early Jewish history was by *visual methods*. They were even more modern than "modern" for their visual religious education included house decorating (vv. 8,9) and symbols to be worn, as well as rituals to be performed. Even their rituals were to be performed in the home where the children were. Their purpose in all these methods was to create curiosity of motivation in the child so that he would ask the questions about God that the parents hoped he would ask. In the future "when your son asks you, What is the meaning of the stipulations . . . tell him . . . Before our eyes . . . God helped us" (Deut. 6:20, 22). They knew that God not only *made* their environment, He wanted to *be* their environment.

Modern parents say that such home teaching was easy in the olden days when the home was the natural center of life and when there were so few outside distractions. But looking back or excusing ourselves does not help our situation. Most of our frustrations today come from meeting present problems with a nostalgic paralysis instead of using our common sense. We are distracted with things and schedules and methods because we forget that the home is first of all a matter of *relationships*. The young son of a soldier knew this. The little fellow was playing in the hotel lobby where his family was living at the time. Someone said to him, "Isn't it a pity you have no home to play in?" He answered, "Oh, we have a home. We just don't have a house to put it in."

A minister's wife had less discernment. She had been a professional woman in the field of religious education before her marriage. It was natural therefore that she was drawn into church activities more than "housework," although she was conscientious in the affairs of her household. But just before she came to the conference where I met her, she overheard one of the parishioners say something about "the preacher's brats." She was stunned. Could they mean her children? They did! This opened her eyes to problems on her own doorstep to which she had been blind before. She now saw that her children had deep rebellion against the church. She faced the fact that the most frustrating hours of the day were just before the children left for school in the morning and after their return in the afternoon. She realized now that the morning hour was the favorite telephone hour for the women of the church because they were sure she was still at home then. No wonder the children felt that the church was in competition with them for the attention of their parents. They felt neglected and unloved. No wonder they rebelled against this intrusion.

After this mother saw where she had failed her children she took drastic steps to correct the situation. She frankly told her Sunday school class of women that she had overheard the "brat" story. She thanked them for awakening her to her responsibilities. She asked the ladies to help her turn the minister's "brats" into the minister's children. The new rule was that no one was to call her in the morning before the children left for school except in case of fire or death! The same rule held for the afternoon hour when the children returned from school. These hours were to be the "children's hours" without any competition.

In these days of compelling interests outside the home, it is a comfort to remember that it isn't so much the *amount* of time a family spends together than makes the difference, as it is what happens when they are together. Ten hours with a distracted, frustrated mother are worse for a child than one hour filled with loving understanding and joyous companionship. This brings to my mind a very likeable young man who was in my class at seminary about a decade ago. He was an athlete, outstanding enough to be chosen for a world tour, but he gave up athletics as a profession to become a minister.

In one of his papers he wrote this about his family: "I have always depended upon God for strength and security and have always tried to do His will. I attribute the attitudes I have to my home environment. My father is the greatest person in the world. I know no other person who is so versatile, so authoritative, so secure, so sensible, so much at home with himself as my father. I would say that my mother has been the real spiritual backbone of our family. My sister and I were born in the depression. My father was principal of a high school at the depression salary of $640.00 a year. At the same time he was working for his master's degree. . . . From the time I was a first grader Dad farmed one hundred and thirty acres, he and mother both taught school, sometimes twenty miles away, and they were part-time pastors of a church forty miles away.

"With planting, plowing, harvesting, paper grading, class parties, funerals, revivals, weddings and preaching we had a merry time. Mother always had time to check our ears for cleanliness. She always seemed to give us each special attention. Dad always found time to shoot baskets with my brother and me in the barn at chore time. Most of all they found time for family worship. I've seen my father keep men waiting in order to take time for worship with the family. They were always invited in to worship and to eat with us if they would come. Mother wanted everyone to stay to eat and Dad would call on the guest to give thanks. I am ashamed to say that I laughed to myself more than once at a plumber or a salesman as he stuttered a prayer. I want to say that a fellow never forgets such things."

Parents indeed hold the key to the atmosphere of the home. If the *peace* of God in their hearts holds against all pressures from without, all frustrations, all differing opinions and family emergencies, then their children will also learn to know this same peace. They will know that this peace cannot be broken by any outside influence. The children will also experience a sense of *security* as the family relationships are strengthened by difficulties met together. This will help them to know that their security is in these close relationships rather than in things. This stable security of the home relationship will bear fruit in a healthy *courage* that cannot be broken by any untoward or cruel experience in the world outside the family. Courage keeps the heart's door open for *hope* even in the darkness of this world. Hope means that there is a *faith* that "this is my Father's world." This faith keeps one's response always toward the God of love. If the child knows that the God of love is the God of his parents he will never lose his courage, but will find it strengthened and preserved so that he can be set *toward* life and not against it.

Unfortunately this is not the experience of every child, even those from homes recognized as religious homes. Several years ago the front page of our evening paper carried a picture of a man with a face so troubled I did not recognize Ron (not his name) at first. The world was shocked because a minister was taken from the pulpit to be put in jail. My heart broke for him and for his good wife because I knew what was back of this tragedy, a minister stealing tools to be able to help boys have good interests in life! This is the story behind the newspaper version: Ron wanted to be a good boy. He loved Sunday school and asked for baptism when he was six years old and was accepted. His father was a proud minister with a hot temper. Any misdemeanor brought punishment to the child after this for "inconsistency." In fact, Ron told me he was punished daily until he graduated from high school. His father never seemed to have any forgiveness for him. A great guilt grew in him and all his childhood faith in God was swept away. He said, "The dilemma of a delinquent son is most difficult, but when a father, although a preacher, is strict and fierce in all family relations the dilemma is one thousand times worse." A ray of hope came from a missionary home on furlough. "He thought I was a good kid, but he went away," Ron said. The glimmer of new courage went with the missionary. Ron added, "The dilemma grew and spread through my whole being like a rabid disease. The virus of failure, indifference and wrongdoing went wild."

There was no prayer at home and the church was no help because Ron could not forget that his father was a preacher. In high school he hunted again for the light. He tried to pray, he took long walks and sang hymns to himself, but he "ended up lost." He said, "My father was right; he said I was a 'throwback to Satan.' I would never amount to anything." (His father was completely wrong. He did not know or live the love of a forgiving heavenly Father.) In spite of all this there was another turning to the light and a desire "to be good" and to keep other boys from trouble, so Ron became a preacher. He wanted to be a good one who would show the way of a loving forgiveness through the grace of God, but he missed the way. I do not know why the warp in his nature was not healed. I only know I feel like praying with our Lord on the cross, "Father, forgive them, for they know not what they do."

The warping of Ron's life by his vindictive father does not necessarily prove that an unfortunate childhood automatically means a twisted adult life. One day in a group of young mothers we were discussing the tremendous importance of the early home life of a child. After class one sweet, young mother, a minister's wife, said to me, "Then is there no hope for me? I had a terrible childhood without love or God in it." My heart sank when I realized what we had done to her. Our emphasis had been intended for her in the role of a young mother. I did not know that any young mother present had been an unloved child. Since that day I can never speak of the importance of a good childhood in the home without adding that at *any age* anyone can start anew and God *can compensate for any lost childhood experience of Him.* Anyone can be converted and become as a little child and enter the kingdom of heaven (Matt. 18:1,2). *Only hopeless despair and a blaming of others can keep anyone from finding a full life in God.*

This fact of God's penetrating, searching love was verified in the life of another young man who had a wretched childhood. He was passed around from relative to relative. Some were religious, but that did not help him any more than it helped Ron. Everywhere he was an added burden, an unwanted nuisance. One woman loved him but could not keep him, another almost loved him but hurt him the most. He was labeled "the little devil" so often he thought he was really a son of the devil. So he prayed to the devil while others prayed to God. I did not know at all about his childhood until one day in class, jokingly, I asked him if he was the "devil's advocate." I did not think of the devil any more than we think of dogs when we eat hot dogs! This took him back to his childhood and he told me his story. It was hard to forgive myself for bringing back even unwittingly a childhood hurt that he tried so hard to forget. But even through this experience a child so sinned against found as an adult that his blighted childhood was no argument against him. This young man is now indeed the "Lord's advocate."

There are too many human repair jobs waiting to be done because there are not enough parents who know the importance of little things, even in a good home, for the development of each child. Some of these occasions are unexpected emergencies in the home, but some of them are expected. The happiest of these expected occasions is the coming of a new baby. But some mothers forget what might happen to other children already in the home. The mother in the home carries the special responsibility for making this a growing experience for all and a blight to none. The joyous results of such thoughtfulness impressed us anew as we read a letter from our daughter-in-law, Kathy, some years ago. She wrote us a report of their sixth child, our thirteenth grandchild. She wrote, ''It's high time I'm writing a full report of your newest granddaughter. What a precious little one she is! Kevin (3½) says her eyes are like two little blueberries. The most common expression around here is, 'Can I hold her?' Next most common would be, 'When will she wake up?' As you can imagine she is very popular with the others. Becky (9) is really big enough to be a help. Krista (5) can hardly keep her hands off her. David (7) holds her very quietly and beams, notices the little toe nails and eyelashes. Kevin's responsibility is to put lotion on her little feet after her bath, which he takes very seriously and does very slowly and carefully. Joyanna (2) is amazingly gentle with all her pats and kisses. How we are enjoying each one. When a new little one is given it is so special it makes all the others special all over again.''

I confess to being proud of this new grandchild but I also rejoice in a daughter-in-law who, as mother to our grandchildren, prepared the other five for the coming of this new baby! The old routines of a home are disrupted by the coming of another, but such a disruption can be a happy one—like Christmas. I will discuss in chapter 7 in more detail how Kathy prepared Becky, her first child, for the coming of the new baby. For now it is enough to see how a thoughtful mother has made a disruption in a family a growing experience for everyone.

The family experience is the training ground for the experience of being a member of the family of God, the household of God, which is the church. Now we must consider the responsibility of the church toward these same children. It is a unique experience for those from good homes. It is a double responsibility for those who have not had a good home life. For the neglected child, it is imperative that the church make up for this love the child may not have ever known and for which love is due to every one.

Homework for Parents—

- Parents, how is your faith in God applied to home relationships?
- Does your relationship to one another set the tone for the children that would indicate the presence of Christ?
- Make a list for one week of your children's comments about their reactions to your actions. Consider the validity of their comments, for their sakes as well as yours.
- Consider the relationship of your daily conversation to the deepest desires of your heart for your children.
- Since the home is the smallest but most important social unit in the world, how does your home rate as a training center for the larger fellowship in the family of God?

Chapter 3

Your Child in the Church

Too many adults think of the church as an institution for adults only. Of course, the children's department is a good place to entertain the children and to park them while the parents "worship." But if the church is "God's household, which is the church of the living God" (1 Tim. 3:15), then it is for the *whole family*. Since the family is society's most important social unit, it carries a great responsibility for its part in the household of God. And the larger family, God's family, will be concerned about every family.

As the family is the custodian of a child's response to God, the church also has its unique responsibility to the children. The church must finish what the family cannot do and it must compensate for wherever the family fails the children. Even when the home is all it should be, the time comes when the parents cannot push a child into the church, the church must *draw* him. The Sunday school teachers, the pastor, and other members of the church must truly represent the drawing power of God's love in their every relationship with every child. The host of little ones are not to be merely tolerated and somehow controlled in the stampede between Sunday school and the worship hour. When the big folk remember that the little ones are the important future members of the church they will recognize them as important individuals to be *noticed* as human beings with their own individual dignity.

Representing God in His love for the children to draw them into His family is much more than decorating the church attractively in order to give a child a "happy experience" during his hours there. If it is only a "happy experience" that is being planned for the child then the day may come when he will decide that he is "happier" elsewhere. On this basis the church will lose out in the competition with those who make a business of entertainment. The church is not in the entertainment business. It is the body of Christ on earth and must do for the children what Jesus did when He was on earth. This means a very *special concern for each child,* for each child is very important to our living Lord. The church is *people* who make up the body of Christ. It is an institution only for loving efficiency. Any family needs organization. The church family has interpretations of theology and doctrines just as a good home has stated beliefs for their deepest convictions. But above all the church is a *relationship* of many people together with their Lord whom they love and worship.

Children understand relationships, especially if they are loving relationships. Perhaps a child has known love at home, perhaps he has not. Since every child is important, those responsible for him in the church will learn to know his family. They will know if his relationship between home and church is a difficult one. If religion is an integral part of everyday life in the home, as it should be, the child will feel at home with the teachers at church who speak the same language. But many children come to the Sunday school as religious illiterates. One young fellow knew so little that when he heard for the first time the wonderful story of the baby Jesus he said, ''Ain't it a pity that they named Him a cuss word?''

A church school teacher frequently meets another even more knotty problem. After children go to school they are often bewildered by new and sometimes contradictory interpretations of the great facts of life and history. One boy was greatly distraught by the creation story. His parents had told him the Genesis story, but his school teacher explained the details of creation in an entirely different way. He loved his parents and his teacher too. But he was about to decide against his parents and the Bible story because of his teacher's persuasiveness— besides there was his interesting new science book. This boy was fortunate to have a real arbiter in his church school teacher, whom he loved. She knew how important it was for this child to keep his faith in the Bible as God's Word. She wanted him to keep confidence in his parents and their faith in God, but she also wanted him to be open to any truth that science might find out about God's world. She told him that the most important thing in the Genesis story was *''In the beginning God created. . . .''* His science book was trying to find out more about *how* God created everything. Scientists change their views frequently as they learn new things about God's universe, but *God in the beginning* remains an unchanging fact. This little boy's world was set straight again because a Sunday school teacher understood him and his problem.

One act of special concern can work miracles in the personality of even the most difficult child. A junior class in a Chicago church was disrupted every Sunday by one unruly boy. The teacher was in despair. Was her first responsibility to this boy or to the others in the class who were hindered from having a good class session? Finally she went to the superintendent who said the class should not suffer and that the unruly boy was to be told to stay at home. Somehow the devout teacher could not settle for that. She was too concerned about the boy. She could not bring herself to tell anyone to stay away from God's house. As a last resort she asked the boy, who was brilliant, to come to her home the next Saturday to help her get some materials ready for Sunday's lesson. He came gladly without embarrassment and gave real help. From that time on he was an asset in the class and never a hindrance. When I heard this story he was superintendent of the Sunday school and a real leader in the church. Not every child with a problem can be won so quickly, but in any case he must be understood as Jesus would have understood when He was on earth, and as He seeks to do *through us* now.

It is only when we have God's understanding concern for all children that the church can truly be the family of God. Even the children who feel a part of the family may be pushed out when we fail to understand them. I remember one preacher's son who knew more Bible than any teacher he ever had. He could pull the rug out from under any poorly prepared Sunday school teacher. In fact, until he was a junior, many of his teachers were afraid of him, as well as being in despair about many of his distracting stunts. One Sunday he helped in the worship service in a beautiful manner, then after prayer threw his Bible across the room. Another time he played a violin solo with amazing skill, but he lay down on his back on the platform to do it! Every teacher said, "I don't know what to do!" One Sunday the juniors were to help in the opening worship of the church service. If only the preacher's boy could be the one to read the Scripture. He was by far the best reader in the department. But what might he do, even in the pulpit, at the morning worship hour? One teacher loved him dearly in spite of his unpredictability. She said, "I think this will be different. His attention-seeking stunts have been with other children. This is with adults and since he will be taking the part of an adult, I think he will behave." That teacher's faith was justified for he behaved most reverently in the pulpit that day. This lad is now grown and is serving and behaving in a pulpit of his own.

When school and other activities increase for young people, church interests seem to compete with these other interests and the church often loses out entirely. This is partly because they do not see the relevance of the church to these other growing interests, but it may also be because no one in the church is involved with them in athletics and their other interests. The church cannot *command* their attention or their attendance. But it can *draw* them back into the church family with understanding love, attention to their interests, genuine fellowship with them. Only love can take this much time for others. And only love draws.

We had a wonderful transformation like this in our church in Chicago a number of years ago. A group of our junior high boys had lost their interest in the church. Many other matters absorbed them. They still came to church, but they sat in the back row of the balcony and paid little attention to the service. Most of them were members of the church, but they did not feel a part of it. Then another young man appeared in their midst. He was one of the top basketball stars in the United States and was then studying to be a minister. He was to be the new teacher of this class. The boys were so excited because he was interested in them. They felt humble, too, and they would not miss a class session. He won the boys, not only for himself, but for the church and for God. It was a red-letter Sunday when the whole group moved from the back row of the balcony to the front rows of the church, right in front of the minister. More than that, by this time they felt at home in those front seats. The rest of the young people soon joined them there and to this day the young people keep those seats filled.

One Sunday after that, as our communion service time was drawing near, these same boys wanted to help in the preparation. In our church we have feet washing and a meal before the communion service. Often boys of this age feel more self-conscious than worshipful in the first part of this ritual, so they shy away from the whole service. Now they were interested enough to help prepare for it. The deacons' wives allowed the boys to wash all the dishes needed for the meal. There was never such a dishwashing! The boys lined up from sink to cupboard and every dish was thrown like a ball from boy to boy. God bless those wonderful deacons' wives! They did not get nervous and, miraculously, not a dish was broken. Nothing could have kept those boys from the communion service. They entered into every part of the liturgy with deep reverence. By helping they had become a real part of the church family.

No matter what any teacher or any other member of the church does to win the children in the church, the rest of the way is blocked unless the minister himself also understands and loves the children. The minister carries a great responsibility in creating the proper image of the church in the mind of the child. In fact, sometimes to the child, he is the church. Out of my childhood I remember one minister we children considered perfect. He looked like the pictures of Jesus. He had the kindest voice and twinkling eyes. We would drop anything to be present when he came to visit. He visited mostly with our parents but by smile and looks he always let us children know that we were included. We felt blessed when he came and we felt like being good children. We loved to hear him preach too, and we listened to every word, whether we could understand it or not.

Some ministers, however, do not know how important the children are to the church. One minister refused to permit the showing of a film at a workers' conference in his church because it depicted a minister taking time out from other duties to sit on a stone fence to talk about the church to a nine-year-old boy. He said, "I have no time for children. Others in the church can do that." He must have cut out of his Bible the things Jesus said about children. Another minister announced open house for the renovated parsonage, then added, "But don't bring any children along. We don't want the parsonage spoiled, and they get on my nerves." Needless to say, the parents stayed away too. How can a child keep responding to the ministry of the Word when the minister talks like that in their hearing?

A minister cannot be like the brash salesman who says, "Win the child and get the mother." A child always discerns ulterior motives. The minister must truly love the children. If he does not have much love for children he can do something about it. One minister I know well came to the realization that he did not feel at ease with the children in his congregation. He decided to spend some time each Sunday in the primary department of the Sunday school. But Sunday after Sunday he would go half-way down the steps to the department and find a block within himself. Before he knew it, he would be coming up the stairs. This puzzled him until he realized that he did not know the children of the church even though he had been their pastor for three years. He decided he must learn to know each child individually. This became a great adventure in his life. *An answering smile from a child became a spiritual experience to him.* The children began to share their art work with him and they introduced him to their dolls and dogs. Little Nancy, who would go to no one outside her family, came to him at church one day and was delighted to be lifted into his arms. They laughed together and talked a little bit before he set her down. Just then Nancy's father came over with a big grin on his face and said, "If I hadn't seen it I wouldn't believe it." This minister had found a real joy in going to the primary department and having some worship with the children. In receiving the children this minister found that he had truly received the Lord Jesus in a new way (Matt. 18:5).

The church's best work has been with the *small* child, but the concern now is just as great for the older child and the youth. All kinds of activities are planned and youth camps are everywhere, but still many churches have to beg the young people to avail themselves of these opportunities. Some say, "They just want a happy time. They aren't interested in the church." But the youth say, "We don't have to be entertained. They think we aren't serious. They bother about the wrong things. We don't need more activities. We need to know about life."

Even juniors like to be a part of the whole fellowship. Long ago I gave up giving a special message to children before I was to speak to adults. (I am not discrediting those who do. We each have our own ways to serve in the kingdom.) Now I find that the children listen through to the end. I would rather have a ten-year-old say, "I understood what you said and I liked it," than to have any praise from his parents. I am still astonished at a thirteen-year-old boy who shook my hand vigorously after I had talked on the church in the world today and said, "You sure were on my beam today. Thank you!" I have seen young people come every night for a week to hear talks on the Holy Spirit or other phases of our Christian living. One thirteen-year-old boy persuaded his parents to let him come every night, instead of sticking to their rule of going out twice a week during school. He said to his mother, "The Holy Spirit will help me do my school work as soon as I get home." His mother permitted him to come. His bright eyes and his alert listening every night are still an inspiration to me.

Many youth raised in Christian homes have problems of guilt and unforgiveness that they cannot handle. They want to know how to get along with their parents. They want to know how to be a Christian on a date. They worry about the Trinity and other theological questions. They wonder how they can know the will of God, how to pray, how to understand the Bible. They are often worried about science and their faith. Many ask, "Is it God talking to me or is it just my desires?" In their hearts they wonder about all the things that have bothered man from the beginning. They are often more serious than their elders. And they are more serious at a younger age than we think. Do not underestimate these little ones (see Matt. 18:10).

There is nothing in the world so relevant to these searchings of our youth as the Good News of Jesus our living Lord. There is nothing so pertinent for every inner yearning as the Holy Spirit, who is the practical part of the Trinity. There is nothing that can keep us from being undermined by fear in this frightened world like knowing God, the Creator of the world, who is our own heavenly Father. God, forgive us for the times we have failed to communicate Your message to these "little ones." Bless *every member* of the household of God, old and young.

Homework—

- *Teachers:* Find the background of each child you teach so that you can know him better. Some teachers keep a secret file for each child and keep a record of every response and every problem.
- *Ministers:* Do the little children know you? Do they feel at ease

with you? Do the youth trust you? Have you taken advantage of the great opportunity in ''membership classes''?
■ *All church members:* Do you know you are part of the family of God? Do you have care and love for all the little ones? What about your conversation in the presence of any ''little ones''?

Chapter 4
The Christian Educator's Dilemma

Little Jimmy hadn't heard many adult theological words even though his parents were faithful in teaching their children about God. One day Jimmy went with his playmate to a children's Bible class. That night after he had prayed he turned to his father and said, "Daddy, *sin, what is it? Am I supposed to do it or not?*"

Jimmy is not alone in his bewilderment. Many adults also are bewildered about words and their meanings. Conflicts come over the *words* of God when we forget the *Word* of God—Jesus Christ, who came to tell us that religion is first of all a *relationship*. The words are important too, and we must soon learn to understand them. However, in New Testament times theological words came *after* an experience of a relationship with God. The words were an attempt to explain what God had done in their lives. Trouble comes when the words pour out in torrents *before* the experience of God. Although in teaching we have to use words, we will be less bewildered if we recognize how little people have when they have *words only* (teaching content) and when we realize how important it is to wait for the "work of grace" in each life. When the teaching is a part of experience then the *same words can have their real meaning.*

By the time the church has a chance at the children the teaching is necessarily more formal. The children are so many and the time is so short. No matter how good the teaching it can never substitute for the unconscious and informal learning of the home. One hour out of 168 a week isn't much, but it is something; and if the child has little or no help in understanding the things of God at home the Sunday morning hour is all the more important. Even one hour a week may be far from futile. The powerful influence of the love of God experienced one hour a week is often great enough to outweigh 167 hours of darkness in a depressing home experience. Let the light shine in darkness and the darkness will not be able to put it out! (See John 1:5.)

After many years of careful planning the church still has to depend almost entirely on volunteer help. Volunteer help is usually untrained help. Some of this volunteer teaching has been haphazard, some of it has been without vision, much of it has been without training or understanding of educational methods. Only in recent decades has there been appreciation in the church of a child's development from one age to another and the consequent adjustment in methods to meet his learning needs. Nevertheless, no statistics can record the influence for God on thousands of children who have been with consecrated teachers who loved God and the children. No matter how little these teachers knew of the "best methods" they came nearer to substituting for the missing Christian influence of the home than any other phase of church life could do.

Organizing for religious teaching through the Sunday school movement developed somewhat the way Topsy grew. Local Sunday school unions began in Philadelphia in 1791. The American Sunday School Union was formed in 1824. It was strictly a layman's movement and no clergy were permitted on the board. The International Sunday School Association, a popular movement, was formed in 1905. In 1910 professional religious educators, concerned about the educational standards of the movements, formed the Sunday School Council of Evangelical Denominations. Tensions rose among the bodies, but concern for the cause was stronger, and the last two bodies merged to form the International Council of Religious Education in 1922. Other combinations and mergers have been made since. Again a group of concerned Christian leaders met to counter certain trends they feared. In 1945 in Chicago they organized the National Sunday School Association. Their slogan was: *Revitalize the Sunday school.* They set out to revive the old Sunday school convention. Their first convention was held at Moody Church in Chicago in October, 1946, with delegates from thirty-five states and two provinces in Canada. This association is in the stream of the National Association of Evangelicals.

In reviewing the religious education movements in the church I am always impressed by the unswerving devotion of the "conservatives" and the intense desire for intellectual honesty of many of the so-called "liberals." The "evangelicals" have never questioned the authority of God, the saving grace of Jesus Christ, man's absolute need of salvation and the Bible as the revelation of God's Holy Word, but they have sometimes forgotten about God's love. (Study the letter to the church at Ephesus in Rev. 2:2–5.) Many who did leave the path of traditional belief in the name of intellectual honesty were restless because they discerned some kind of lack and if they remain intellectually honest they would have to find this lack. Their honest search was an exciting adventure. They took cues from new educational and scientific discoveries and set out to organize the church for the best teaching methods possible. In *following* secular educational methods they fell prey to fads that were no help to the spiritual development of the church. Then they saw that through the neglect of ''content'' they had neglected the facts of the story of God's revelation to man as recorded in the Bible, they had lost the stabilizing security of traditional observance and the discerning perspective of history. Now the real test of intellectual honesty came as they returned to temporarily discarded values, now more precious than ever. Others became as defensive of their departure from tradition as some were who never departed! Oh, that we might see each other as God sees us!

Before there were any divisions in the Sunday school movement a Sunday school tradition developed, and any deviation from this traditional format was feared. This greatly impeded progress in the educational work of the church. The original clerical opposition to the Sunday school movement, a layman's movement, helped to create a wall between the Sunday school and the church. Many pastors are still expected to keep hands off the Sunday school. This separation developed into a dual standard of music and worship. There were Sunday school songs and church songs, which required different song books. Large Bible classes often made the church a separate side show in some city churches. One Sunday school teacher in a large Chicago Bible class bemoaned the fact that many of his class left before church service began, satisfied with their class activities. He, as well as the minister, wanted them to be a part of the larger fellowship. They both wanted the Sunday school to be a training medium for the church rather than an end in itself.

In the early days everyone studied the same lesson with no planned grading for different age groups. Those who knew how to talk to children in simple language got along better than the good souls who studied the lesson carefully, so they thought of the lesson only. Many were satisfied if they got through the lesson without too much noise from the children. Even then, some taught *children* and some taught the *lesson,* but very few knew how to teach the *lesson* to the *children.* As educators began to realize how a child learns and what he can learn best at different ages they adapted the church's teaching to the child's understanding, and so *graded lessons* came into being.

Years ago there was little understanding of the "age of accountability," although this expression was used often. An immature child, immature only because of his age, was often considered on a par, especially at revival meeting time, with the hardened sinner who had deliberately turned from God. Christian educators who loved children began to wonder: Why should a child ever turn from God? Couldn't he be led to love God from the very first days of his understanding? But if he always loved God and never turned from Him, then would he need a conversion experience? In answering these questions many religious educators lost their way for awhile. They had to learn the difference between the conversion of the rebellious sinner and the conversion of the child who never rebelled but who still had to decide, as he became "accountable," whether he would obey or rebel. His decision for his life must be just as definite as that of the "sinner" who turns *back* to God. They have now both chosen the same path, the same commitment to the Savior. The preparation or nurturing the child for this *choice* became the responsibility of every Christian dealing with a child. This preparation for "accountability" meant that the child would learn the disciplines of life that would help him be responsible in carrying out the choices he would make.

With the better understanding of a child's developmental process of growth the church educational program became a "child-centered" program. In fact, the program became so child-centered that the goal of the training was often forgotten. Jesus put a child in the midst, it is true, but He did not make the child the whole show. In homes and churches the problem doubled whenever all sense of "authority" went out the window, and the child was given leeway for *self-expression* before he had developed a *self* to express. The "new" thinkers believed that a nice environment would do the trick for the development of personality. *Good* and *bad* became naughty words for parents and teachers to use to or about children. Many forgot that discipline is basically directive and so all restraint was frequently removed.

When educators realized that their "child-centered" program tended toward making "*self*-centered" children they then had to do something to get a child's attention off himself. As a result they instituted the popular *project method*. The project was now the center of attention. Any resources necessary for the completion of the project were used. The Bible was a resource, subsidiary to the project. Anything else needed was just about as important as the Bible. It didn't make much difference, just so the *project* was completed. So it turned out that the *project* became an end in itself.

As the loopholes in the project method appeared, a synthesis of the child-centered program and the project method was found. This was called the *life-situation* method. This became the "problem-centered" era. At that time someone facetiously said of a certain minister, "Without a problem spake he not unto them."

By the late 1920s many devout Christian educators who knew the Lord began to feel a great fear; far too many church members looked on the church as merely an extra organization. There was little consciousness of the authority of God or any other authority. Then came the depression, and in another decade another world war. Man's overconfidence in the natural goodness of man and his underconfidence in a personal God, the Creator of the Universe, brought darkness to his soul as he realized anew the final helplessness of man. Even churchmen cried, "Oh, that I knew where I might find Him!" Someone said in that dark day, "It seems that religious educators know how to teach anything, but they do not have anything to teach."

It was another decade and a half before many religious educators could bring themselves to accept the "old-fashioned" idea of the grace of God and to incorporate this truth with the best methods they had learned. As one educator said, "It is again respectable to believe in the grace of God!" After many wars and much moral decay throughout the land, men now know they have need of God and a power higher than man's power. The educational wing of the church is again generally a recognized evangelistic agency to prepare youth to know the God who is ever seeking them.

With all the lessons learned through experience by all God's people there are still some important ones we have been slow to learn. Jesus' yearning prayer for His disciples then and now is: "Holy Father, protect them by the power of your name—the name you gave me—so that they may be one as we are one" (John 17:11). Also, "A new command I give you: Love one another. As I have loved you, so you must love one another. All men will know that you are my disciples if you love one another" (John 13:34,35). When we do not love, it is the children in our homes, in our churches, and in our world who lose their way and stumble because of us.

Jesus used the same Scriptures that the "churchmen" of His day revered, but Jesus had to reject the majority of interpretations they made. He saw the Word of God they could not discern, so He charged, "You have let go the commands of God and are holding on to the traditions of men" (Mark 7:8). We need to ask again and again, "Are we preserving *orthodoxy,* but losing all spiritual meaning?" We have not fought over Jesus Christ, we love Him—or think we do. It is our *interpretations* of our Lord and His Words that get us into trouble with one another and with Him. If we are satisfied with mere indoctrination, then we have failed in the greatest gift of salvation, which is reconciliation with God and true abiding relationship with Him. We need deeper meanings of *conversion,* which is more *to Someone* than *from some condition.*

If we have emphasized a certain kind of emotional experience as conversion rather than establishing a living relationship with Christ, which grows in daily experience, then we have caused many to stumble as they try to hold a certain "feeling" they once had. This new relationship with God is more faith than feeling. Children *must be prepared* for this understanding of what happens in conversion. Most young people are as little prepared for an experience of the love of God as they are for real love in marriage.

In Jesus' day the children never felt excluded from Him. In His presence they always felt a warm welcome. They were never outsiders. To please our Lord today we must bring the children inside and keep them from wanting to go outside. They must be nurtured to love Him. Then as they grow older and their horizons widen and they see other ways, they must be nurtured to *want to* choose Him and His way. After they choose His way and accept Him as their Savior they must be nurtured to grow in Him and His way in every phase of life. I still remember my mother's daily prayer, "Help us to bring up our children in the nurture and admonition of the Lord." As a child I heard the phrase so often I thought it was one big word: "nurtureandadmonition." Now I know it has a lifetime of big meaning.

I heard one time that some people are afraid of the word "nurture." Really, it is as old-fashioned and as biblical as the Proverb (22:6 King James) "Train up a child in the way he should go, and when he is old he will not depart from it." More and more responsibility is being laid at the door of parents for the outcome of their children. Many people say our problem is delinquent parents, not delinquent children. This proverb on *training, educating* or *nurturing* children is being reinterpreted for our day of much more complicated living. We can easily see where the emphasis on authority for authority's sake had its shortcomings. The child who was "punished into shape" obeyed until he could break away, so little of character value occurred in his personality. Educators who understood a child's development saw what was happening in the life of the child who had no chance to learn to think for himself. For a period of years many went too far the other way, ignoring all authority and even directive restraint. Then it had to be admitted that a child had less security and sense of direction with too little authority than he had with too much authority. Parents can be very happy that we are now in a period of synthesis between these two extremes. Now we are set free to find out why so many children departed from the way in which their parents thought they had trained them.

We must therefore think anew about the real meaning of *training* or *educating* a child so that the training will hold as the biblical proverb says it will. The Hebrew word *hanakh* used here and translated *train up* or *educate* means *to dedicate*. It is from the same root word as Hanukkah. The feast of Hanukkah celebrates the rededication of the temple in Jerusalem under the Maccabees in 165 B.C. Could we say then that this proverb infers that training or educating is *to dedicate to God?* Because of the Hebrew word used for the child and for the temple, perhaps the Jews of Jesus' day thought of dedication to God in each case. And perhaps Jesus thought of the dedication of His life when He said, "Destroy this temple, and I will raise it again in three days" (John 2:19). John says, "The temple he had spoken of was his body."

Paul continued the idea of the body as a temple: "Don't you know that you are God's temple and that God's Spirit lives in you?" (1 Cor. 3:16), and "Do you not know that your body is a temple of the Holy Spirit, who is in you, whom you have received from God? You are not your own; you were bought at a price. Therefore honor God with your body" (1 Cor. 6:19,20).

Perhaps this will give us our cue to escape from the dilemma about *education* and *grace*. Training or learning *before* "grace" is a preparation of the temple of the body (meaning the *whole* person in the Bible) for confrontation with God at the time of accountability. It is the preparation of a place for His Spirit to dwell. The preparation of the body, mind, heart, spirit, for God to come in, involves one's capacity for love, for faith, for choice, for dependability in *response*.

After his physical birth into this natural world the child must then be cared for in preparation for his spiritual birth into the kingdom of God. From birth to rebirth may be called the *spiritual prenatal period*. We cannot educate *into* faith but we can educate in preparation *for* faith. We do not naturally grow *into* grace, but we can be prepared to receive this great gift from God so that we can grow *in* it. Many educators have failed because they thought that everything depended on *man's efforts;* others failed because they thought everything depended on *God's part* in our lives. God's Word teaches us that God limited Himself in creation by giving man the power of choice. God always does His part, we must learn to do our part in responding to Him. Then the Christian educator's dilemma will be solved.

Homework for Parents and Teachers—

■ As parent or teacher, "Do your best to present yourself to God as one approved, a workman who does not need to be ashamed and who correctly handles the word of truth" (2 Tim. 2:15).

- How many of your "spiritual difficulties" come from immature capacities in your life?
- Test your "convictions" (see 1 John 4:1): "Do not believe every spirit, but test the spirits to see whether they are from God. . . ."
- List the things you are "sure" of. Did you get them from your background only, or have they been tested through God's spirit? Even if all are of God, have you made them truly your own?
- Test your attitude toward those who differ from you. Can you love them in the Lord? Can you learn anything from them?

Chapter 5

Let the Children Come

A child's experience of God is real. It is as real as the love in his life. The imperfection or immaturity of his image of God is never a hindrance to him unless the image was created by a loved adult. Whenever he realizes that some image he formed himself is wrong or inadequate it is easily sloughed off by the new idea that has come to him. But if a parent or teacher has given him a wrong image his emotions are involved and he has trouble changing.

One of the loveliest stories of a child's experience of God was given to me in the summer of 1942. My roommate at a summer conference had come into a new experience of God the year before, after many years of fruitless seeking. The barren years doubled her appreciation of this newly found joy in the Lord. Nevertheless, the spontaneity of her joy would often suddenly be overtaken by a consuming shyness. If I found her reading her Bible, as she did so much when alone, she would suddenly cover the Book, and then, embarrassed, she would smile and uncover it. One day I said to her, "You know more Bible than any preacher I know. Why are you so shy about something you love so much?" She said, "I never thought of the reason before, but I guess I know it. In fact, I wrote it all down years ago one day when I desperately longed for the God of my childhood. I'll give you a copy, if you want it." This is the beautiful story she gave me, with permission to use it any time:

"I knew God quite well when I was a child. As I grew older it seemed that I was alone and alien in my knowledge. So, ashamed perhaps of that simple intimacy, I left Him; left Him and my rag doll and my playhouse under the great oak tree in the backyard, and ventured forth to search for more acceptable knowledge of Him; a search through discarded scrap heaps and in shining temples. Owners of scrap heap and temple alike welcomed me. 'Here,' they would say, 'is just what you need. Look this way and you will see Him!'

"So many times I have looked—through magnificent prisms,

through bits of crystal picked from the mud under foot. Sometimes I have seen a flare of color. Sometimes I have half believed in a disappearing flash of wings. These latter days I have remembered, with longing, that simple reality of long ago. And I do not believe the green hedge through which I pushed my way to the world outside has grown too thick and high for me to recognize the boundaries of home. . . .

"I was just past six when the big black book in grandmother's bedroom began to exert its secret fascination over me. Anyone seeing her read it would have known that it held some great mystery, some sweet and thrilling knowledge, something more special than even *Alice in Wonderland* or the *Wizard of Oz*. And so the acquisition of its contents became the lodestar of my childhood.

"One day, as I sat on the floor beside grandmother making doll clothes with large darning needle stitches, I worked out a plan of procedure. I had learned my 'a b c's' and I knew that all words were made from them. If I could learn the letters in each word in the big black book and ask different people what they meant, in time I would have learned them all and the secret would belong to me, too.

"A few minutes before lunch I ran down the hill to my own home, tore back to the kitchen and, hot with excitement, demanded of the cook, 'Dora, what does i-n mean?' Dora told me. 'What does t-h-e spell?' Dora told me. That was all I remembered. After lunch I slipped out the door and back to grandmother's, and before mother arrived with an afternoon nap in her voice, I had learned b-e-g-i-n-n-i-n-g and was all primed to find out about G-o-d.

"The last was more difficult because mother told me He was the same Person I had learned about at Sunday school, and the same One to whom I said *Now I lay me* every night. I carefully explained that this was impossible. My Sunday school teacher was a friend of mother's. She told me the exciting stories of *Alice in Wonderland* and the *Wizard of Oz,* and the Sunday story was always about a little boy named Jesus. The Person I said *Now I lay me* to was called Lord. The discovery that the same Person had three names was very disconcerting until I remembered I had three myself.

"I asked no more analytical questions after I had added the remaining words of the sentence. This multi-named Person had created the heaven and the earth. Dora said that meant *made*, just like she made pies and cakes. If He could do that, He could do anything else. God who went around making trees and grass and clouds and stars, and little girls and boys, need not appear visibly in order that I be assured of His identity and reality. Later I was to learn three words about Him: omnipotence, omniscience, and omnipresence—but then I knew their meaning before.

"As time passed, life was not too easy for my family and Dora, but I did learn to read! Abraham, Isaac, Moses, and most especially my dear Joseph of the beautiful coat were ever present, and I held long conversations with God about them. *Cinderella* and *Alice in Wonderland* were just as interesting to God and I wondered why they had been left out of the Book. Perhaps I would come to them later on.

"Sometimes I felt that God and I were the only ones who really loved the Genesis folk. Other people were so strange about them. When the swishy, sweet-smelling ladies came on Friday night to Study Circle someone would always say, 'Now, dear, tell us about the little baby Moses,' or perhaps they would ask about dear Joseph. Before I would be finished they were always smiling; not a love smile like when they hugged me and said, 'How's my girl?' but a laughing queer smile that looked as if it did not belong. And so after a while I hid when the Circle ladies came, and when they would find me and ask about Isaac or Jacob I would feel my face getting redder and redder, and there was nothing I could say.

"There was a big fat lady, who breathed some place way down, who invariably caught me around the waist on such occasions and said, 'The cat's got her tongue.' Her hands were squashy and damp, and she held me fast so I could not move, while she laughed around at the others.

"The climax came one evening just after my seventh birthday. The Circle ladies were all there. Having been scolded time and time again for my brevity of speech in their presence, I determined to answer any question they might ask me.

"The invariable question came, and from the fat lady who breathed from some place way down. 'What are you reading now?' she asked. That was not hard at all. I looked around with a confident air and smiled at mother with assurance that I was going to do the family honor for once. 'The *Plas-sums*,' I announced, meaning *Psalms*. I am told that I was a difficult child and given to storms of temper. The first one that I remember followed the shouts of laughter which my *Plas-sum* statement brought forth. I seized the most available Bible, and there were several, since the Circle ladies were Sunday school teachers and had met to study the weekly lesson. I threw it across the room, slammed the door behind me and retired to the front steps in fury, regardless of consequences. Needless to say, there were consequences.

''Nothing could induce me to touch the big black Book after that episode. Grimm's *Fairy Tales* were boring to a point of insipidity after reading of the lurid Egyptian plagues and rods that turned to serpents. But even if I would not read about them, I had remembered the stories, and when I was sure I was alone under the apple tree in the backyard I would recount them in detail to Lillie John.

''Lillie John was limp and unresponding after the manner of any rag doll, but I loved her dearly. Her face had long since been blotted into blankness by dirt, kisses and the application of brown sugar which I daily achieved from the white jar in the pantry. Lillie John was almost as fond of brown sugar as I was, and she never grew tired of the stories.

''God used to come and sit under the tree with us, too. In fact, He was almost always there, and He loved the stories and our games as much as we did.

''Somewhere along here I learned about heaven. Dora said it was up there just past the blue sky. There were golden streets and angels. Dora said angels were people all dressed up in white with wings so they could go anywhere they pleased. She showed me a picture of the wings in a book, and then one afternoon when I looked up into the sky—there they were, millions of them, so many they were stacked on top of each other, all washed and clean and stretched out to dry. True, it was Friday, and that was not washday with us, but I supposed things were different in heaven.

''The stars puzzled me for a long, long time until one night the simplest of all explanations came to me. Naturally the angels were curious about the people who lived down on the earth. They had simply punched little holes in the floor of heaven so they could peep down and see what was going on. No one would ever have known about it if it had been light all the time, but when darkness came the glittering gold of the heavenly walls and streets just shone right through the little cracks.

"Sundays we did not play in the backyard. Sundays were different. The very minute breakfast was over I had to start standing still. First, my hair was very carefully brushed and curled over mother's left forefinger, and then one of the three special party ribbons was tied on my hair. I wore my best dress with one of the new sashes for my waist, and the stiff pair of shoes that shone. I had a blue pocketbook with embroidery on it. There was a nickel inside for the Sunday school offering and a white handkerchief folded across the middle.

"Daddy always took me home after Sunday school, but one Sunday Mother said, "Would you like to stay to church with us today?' I had often wondered about church, so I said 'yes.'

"There were rows and rows of seats with all the neighbors sitting in them very quiet-like. Up front there was a big high table with Brother Dean sitting behind it. He did not see me, but I felt at home, for he often came to see grandmother. Mr. Allen, who fixed the ice cream sodas at the drugstore, was there behind a brown curtain, and Miss Polly, who hummed little tunes all the time when she came to sew by the day, was sitting with three other people in a row beside him.

"Almost as soon as we sat down, Mr. Allen leaned forward and there was a deep sound of music. It grew and grew and rose to heaven and all the people stood as though they would somehow go there too. I stood on tiptoe to reach after the words which seemed to come from my very own heart, even though I had never heard them before:

> Praise God from whom all blessings flow,
> Praise Him, all creatures here below;
> Praise Him above, ye heavenly host;
> Praise Father, Son, and Holy Ghost.

"I pulled mother down so I could whisper in her ear, 'Is this church, telling God how glad we are just because He is?' And she said it was.

"That was the best part of church. For when Brother Dean stood up front and talked he used a queer sort of voice that I had never heard before, and it seemed as though he did not expect anyone to listen to him. It was not easy to hear him, for all the words seemed to float out the door on a little wave just above my head.

"Not long after that the fairy tale lady who always told about the little boy Jesus on Sunday said that a person called a missionary was going to talk the next afternoon in the Baptist church. That was an old brick building just down the street from home, and not far away like our Methodist one. It gave me an idea. I would go to hear her and I would take God and Lillie John to hear her too.

"It was easy to do. I always played in the backyard in the afternoon and no one called me away until it was time to wash my hands for supper. About the middle of the afternoon we three slipped out the front gate and walked down the street. No one noticed us, and we sat down in the very back seat, for the missionary lady was already talking as we came in. We could see only her face, but it was smily, the sort of smile that mother wore when she rocked me to sleep and like the fairy tale lady smiled when she told me about the Pied Piper and the little boy Jesus. We liked her and listened to every word she said. It was easy to listen because we did not have to reach up to pick her words off that wave in the air. She talked just like Brother Dean did when it wasn't Sunday.

"She had been in a big, big country called China, which was across the ocean. We decided the ocean was bigger than the Red Sea, because it took her two weeks to cross it. The children of Israel got through the Red Sea in almost no time.

"In this country called China there were thousands and thousands of people who did not know about Jesus, and she had been telling them about Him. We were so excited we could hardly sit still, but we could not understand the people who were listening to her. All the Circle ladies who laughed about the Genesis folk and the fat lady who asked about the *Plas-sums* were there, and instead of queer smiles that looked as if they did not belong, there were tears!

"The missionary lady had the same tears in her voice, but she kept on smiling and she was asking if anyone there would go and tell the story about Jesus to the people across the ocean. I thought, of course, the Circle ladies would all say they would go, and I was so glad because that would mean they would not come to Study Circle on Friday nights. But no one moved or said a word.

"There was nothing in the world so exciting or interesting! Why didn't they all say they would go? And why did they cry? We decided for about the fortieth time that grown people were the silliest things in all the world and that we would never grow up.

"When the ladies started going out the door, we went up to the missionary lady and I told her I knew all the stories she had been talking about, and all about the little boy Jesus and heaven and the angels, and that Lillie John, God and I would be very glad to go with her to China, that is, of course, if mother would let us.

"She did not say a word for a long time, just hugged us close and wiped a lot of tears off her face. I thought perhaps I ought to cry too, but I could not although I tried, and thought of all the sad things I knew.

"Finally she stood me on a bench in front of her and looked at me and Lillie John, 'I cannot take you with me now, but perhaps when you are grown God will let you speak for Him somewhere. Meanwhile, you can be a little missionary right where you are.' Then she walked us to the door and asked me where I lived. I showed her the white house up the street. She said she would watch to see that we got home safely.

"We had not been missed and presently we were under the apple tree talking it over. The lady said I could be a little missionary right where I was. Being a missionary meant telling about the little boy Jesus, about Abraham, Isaac, and the dear, dear Joseph of the beautiful coat. We had already told everyone we knew. When we told them they laughed and said, 'Isn't she the quaintest little thing?' When she told them they cried. She had said there were thousands and thousands of people in China. Perhaps that had something to do with it. I asked Dora what thousands and thousands meant. 'Oh, heaps, as many as there are leaves out there on the big oak tree,' she said.

"That did not help, but it did give rise to an idea. The leaves would not laugh. I could play that they were people—people in China, perhaps. So I changed from a lean little girl who played quietly with her doll into a veritable tomboy, a state distressing to my family. My knees were perpetually scratched, hands blackened, dresses torn and my hair bore marks of tree bark in its tangles. Punishment, lectures, admonitions of every kind failed. Regardless of casualties, I continued in the downward path until I had climbed every tree in the frontyard and backyard and had exhausted my supply of stories in each. Such was my missionary career.

"There were other things I learned of God in those days, but I cannot remember them. It has been a long time since I started off alone. Lillie John has gone the way of all rag dolls, but God still waits under the big oak for me. That is the only thing in life of which I am certain. Nor is He far away. The simplicity of the landscape is familiar these days—too familiar, too dear to mistake. Soon—perhaps around the next turn of the road—shall be *home*."

This is Mary Jane's story which she wrote in 1927, but it was fourteen more years before she found the Lord who had been waiting for her all that time.

Of her searching years she said, "It was a night that lasted half a lifetime, but only I knew that it was night and that I was living in it, because the darkness was within me. Stumbling around within myself, for that was where I was, I lashed out at those I thought had taken the light from me, against all that apparently stood between the light and my unhappy self, and I beat upon the doors of heaven as I begged for my sight again."

The light broke through into her dark, empty life in the summer of 1941, and when it came she knew that it was the same light that had made her childhood bright, but now it was an adult light. So important and real was a child's experience of God that it served as a homing beam through so many dark years. Restored sight brought recognition of the Friend of her childhood, now the Lord of all her life.

"Let the children come."

Homework for Parents—

- Find out what your children and other children think about God and Jesus. Really listen to them.
- Gently guide them where they are mixed up.
- Be prepared for surprise and inspiration.

Part II

Preparation for Rebirth

Flesh gives birth to flesh, but the Spirit gives birth to spirit.
John 3:6

Chapter 6
Love for Relationship

"God used to come and sit under the tree with us, too. In fact, He was almost always there, and He loved the stories and our games as much as we did." As we read in the preceding chapter, this was Mary Jane's memory of a beautiful relationship with God in her childhood. It was personal enough to haunt her through the years away from God. Then when the relationship was restored, what a joy it was to her to know that she did not have to go back to her childhood to find Him. He was there at the door of her life waiting for her adult response.

Mary Jane's remembered experience was more than a set of religious rules imposed on a child. Rules and thought patterns can be changed with the years, but any relationship of love holds a corner in the heart forever. Jesus came to earth to reveal to us that the most important fact of true religion is that we can have *relationship* with Him. Since *God is love* this relationship must be one of love.

The average love song gives one the idea that love is for instant happiness. One can "fall in love" and have lots of thrills. The catch is that those who fall in love can just as easily fall out of love. Their *ins* or *outs* are determined by how they *feel*. This kind of love is a self-centered thing: it is "how does he make *me* feel?" It is a one way experience, therefore it is not a relationship experience. When love is a relationship experience it is *outgoing* and never grasping. It is a life adventure to probe the true meaning of love. The discovery comes not through a "fall" but through accepting in mind and heart God's definition of love.

Real love of the quality of God-love is expressed in the Greek by the word *agape*. In the effort to get away from all the disillusionments of man's misconceptions of *love* the word *agape* has become a part of our own language. This love is more than a feeling, it is an attitude; but it is also more than an attitude; it is a genuine quality of life, and a basic one at that. God doesn't merely love us, or *have* love for us, He *is* love. No matter what we are or what we do, we cannot change God or His love for us. *He is still unchanging love.* What He does in relation to us is according to His nature and not according to ours. No matter what happens *God is love.*

Agape is a *giving love* and not a mere *receiving love.* It is not *I want to be loved* but *I love you.* It does not change color under any circumstance or toward any kind of person. It is an outgoing love that always seeks the best for another. It always protects the integrity of another and at the same time makes it possible to preserve its own integrity. This love is never superficial: it is a life decision, a promise maintained only by faith's discipline, a gift of unlimited God-love. The "loved one" is always fortunate, but he who truly loves is "God's own."

It is always startling to us to see how quickly children can discern the connection of love in relationships. Last December eight-year-old Becky and her classmates were decorating their classroom (in a parochial school) for Christmas. They fell into verbal fighting about their plans. Then suddenly one of the children said, "We cannot fight about decorations for Jesus' birthday. We must take the decorations down until we can put them up lovingly." All agreed and down came the decorations they had already put up! That evening Becky came home full of sadness as she told her mother about their experience. The next evening she was still sad. The third evening she came home with a radiant face. "We love each other now and we have decorated our room for Christmas," she reported happily. The season of the celebration of God's love gift to the world meant something to those children.

Even a little touch or a brief experience of *giving love* is something never to be forgotten. One example is a loving mother with her baby, the first or the tenth. My mother's first child died when he was six weeks old. As a young girl I could not understand her grief at this loss, which she often mentioned. How could one love a tiny baby that much? Commensurate with her grief was her joy in my coming two years later. This part of the story I could understand and appreciate: that she wanted me so much. The significance of mother's whole experience came to me when my first baby was to be born. I was surprised to find how much love I had for the little one I could not yet see. If I had any fear at all, it was that I might lose my baby as my mother did. I found that with the baby comes the *inborn* love for it. What does a mother ask but that her baby grow normally? Sleepless nights are no argument against love. One finds that this love is full of care and a new sense of responsibility. One also finds, with surprise, that this love of the little one can obliterate self-concern and self-pity. If only every mother could remember love's lesson of these *giving* years!

Another touch of true *giving love* is the love between a man and a woman when they begin their life together: he would give up the whole world for her, she would forsake all others and all else for him. With this *giving love* experience they find the greatest sense of fulfillment they have ever known. The Christian plan for marriage is that this *giving love* should continue through life. The husband is to love his wife as Christ loves the church. She is to keep herself subject to his best welfare in the Lord. This new sense of life and even freedom should give them the clue that *giving love* is the love that establishes relationship for life. If only every husband and every wife could remember love's lesson of *giving!*

Too often, however, husbands and wives and parents never realize how much their experience of fulfillment comes from what they *give* rather than from what they *try to get*. Then the day too frequently comes when they grasp for love and cease to think of giving it. The man begins to feel "henpecked" and the woman begins to feel "walked over" as if she were a "doormat." Barriers rise and a relationship is cracked or broken. Why are we so blind that we do not see that fulfillment lies in the *giving* and not merely in the *getting*.

Another striking illustration of the hidden power of *giving love* is the annual story of the "Christmas spirit." In spite of commercialism, the burden of an increasing greeting card list and favor-seeking gifts, there is still something that "gets" people as the season comes on. It may be a "Miracle on 34th Street" or even old Scrooge, but something happens inside. If this spirit is uplifting and life-giving at one season of the year, why is it called impractical all the rest of the year?

It may be that part of our blindness to the value of *giving love* in the building up of relationship is that we get lost in the giving of *things*. *Things* can so easily become a substitute for love. Then the *things* become a tool in relationship and an indication of lack of love. Parents who cease to give of themselves to their children may feel some satisfaction from the shower of gifts they bestow, but the children know when a gift is a *substitute* for love instead of a *token* of real love. The child who has received genuine love will never have to look to things as a substitute in his life. A child's security is never in things but in his personal relationships. *Thing giving* may be *love giving,* or it may not, but time will always tell. The child who becomes a commodity for his parents to manipulate with gifts will have a hard time learning to know genuine love as God defines it. God's heart is broken for the millions who do not know genuine love; this is the reason for the cross.

Everyone is born with a *capacity* for love, but it must be developed. For the unfortunate babe the capacity may be smothered before it has a chance to grow. This unfortunate one is just as likely to be in a "good" home as in the slums. The normal outreach of the child is for love and toward love. It is love that draws out the innate desire and satisfies the innate hunger for relationship. It is the parents who give the little one his definitions of and for life.

The new baby can do nothing at first but be a recipient of love and care. Although he has a security in this loving care that he cannot yet comprehend, as the days go by he gradually learns to respond spontaneously. That first smile! That first word! What a thrill to those who love the baby. This response is the first step toward developing a love that can be the capacity in his life for a real relationship with God. Genuine human love prepares the "temple" for divine occupancy. This is what parents must remember.

There is another normal side to a baby's life that we must consider. He *will* have frustrations, and they can be made to serve him in his growth. As he grows he must learn to accept them as a part of life. This may be even in a matter like proper sleep habits. If he learns to take these frustrations, knowing no break in loving relationship, he will feel no loss of security and he will be taking his first step toward developing the capacity for out-going love.

Friends of mine were in a restaurant when a sizable family sat down at the next table. The four-year-old became quite unruly and paid no attention to his parents' correction. The father took the little fellow outside. Sounds were heard! After some time, to the surprise of my friends, when the two returned the little fellow was all smiles. As he sat down at the table he looked around at the family and announced with satisfaction, "Daddy adjusted me!" The rest of that meal was a happy experience for the whole family and an inspiration to those at the neighboring table. One little fellow was learning to cope with and make use of his frustrations!

As the children grow and make more demands, parental love will really be tested as to whether it is genuine *giving love* or only a facsimile. One mother "didn't have the heart to refuse anything her children asked for." In the name of "love" she let them eat anytime they pleased, so they nibbled all the time and had no appetite for balanced meals. Actually this mother wasn't loving, she was lazy and thoughtless and undisciplined. She was hurting her children spiritually more even than physically.

Another test comes to genuine parental love when the child begins to find his own identity. He will begin to separate himself from mother and daddy; he will want to do things on his own. He will often be rebellious, but he will seem more rebellious than he really is. If his parents are wise they will respect his emerging selfhood and will help him take over his controls as fast as he is capable of doing so. If the parents' love is genuine they will avoid emphasizing the budding rebellion and will emphasize the new dignity. They will know what is happening to their child and will not be hurt by what he seems to be doing to them.

Through the parents' love that understands and is always dependable, the child will be ready to learn something about the consistency and the endless patience of the love of God. Through this parental love he will know a disciplined relationship that frees him to understand the love of God that truly sets a man free to be greater than even his highest dreams. Again we can say that the child who is held by *things* rather than by genuine *love* will never know the freedom of personal integrity. (It is perfectly respectable to be five years old when one is five!) The recipient of things turns rebellious and bitter when he does not receive what he thinks he wants. He will be blamed for "ingratitude" and will be helplessly frustrated. The child must experience genuine love from his parents before he can experience it in his own life.

My mail is filled with the tragic accounts of the perversion of love that is called *possessive love*. Sometimes it is facetiously called *smother love!* This makes a child insecure because he is bound by the very person who should set him free. He never knows if his relationship is secure, so he has to play all the time for favor. Even that favor never gives him security for he must always work for more of it. "Mother loves you, do this for her," is never a fair premise for a request. Love asks no returns. Only genuine *giving love* gets genuine returns. *A child has not experienced real love unless he learns to love back.* This is the greatest return of genuine love. It is preparation for understanding that "we love him because he first loved us." It is direct preparation for understanding and having fellowship with God.

One of the greatest evidences of love is the ability to forgive. Even on the cross Jesus prayed, "Father, forgive them, for they know not what they do." Jesus *understood* the people: that they did this cruel thing to Him because of their blindness and weakness. Because He understood He asked the Father to forgive them. He forgave because He was God-love. We fail in God-love, which is not only *giving love* but *understanding love,* when we fail to understand a child and why he acts like he does. The evidence of this failure toward our children is in our tendency to label a child. *Labeling a child means to him that he is not forgiven.* When a child is labeled he does not know what to do but to live up to the label! Many a child has received the push to delinquency from the labeling of some "good" person.

Many acts of unforgiveness go unnoticed because they are so common. A little girl, in an *effort to help* her mother, broke a dish worth much in sentiment and money. A mother, in such circumstance, will be deciding by her reaction what she considers more important: the dish or the child's desire to help. If the latter, she will encourage the child in the helpfulness without too much despair over the dish. Then she will see to it that the little girl will have opportunities to help without harm to mother's valuable possessions. She will never say, "No, you cannot help. You always drop things!" If the child is labeled as a "thing dropper," she will not only feel unforgiven but her desire to help will be hurt. It is also important for the mother to distinguish between accidental deeds and willful deeds, but in either case loving understanding will always show *forgiveness*. How can a child understand the forgiveness of God if he has never had the experience of forgiveness in his home relationships?

When we think of the importance of showing *patient love* to a child, while our lives are so *busy* in this complicated world, it is easy to be filled with anxiety. One conscientious father caught himself self-consciously *trying* to love his children. Then one day, with a smile and a shrug of the shoulders, he said: "I've decided not to try to *love* them. I'm just going to *enjoy* them." Enjoying the children is loving them without the anxiety. This is a wise discernment for a parent because, when there is anxiety, the children seem to pick up the anxiety and miss the attempted love!

Every mother knows how anxiety gets across to children on the days when the work "pushes her" before the arrival of guests. "They played outdoors so happily yesterday, why are they underfoot today?" The fact is they are seeking an assurance of relationship. Mother's anxiety makes them feel uneasy. They don't know what is the matter. She gains no time by pushing them away. She will gain time if she will take them up and "hug them good" as if she had nothing to do all day but love them. With this assurance of her love they will feel free to run out to play.

"There is no fear in love, but perfect love casts out fear, because fear has to do with punishment. The man who fears is not made perfect in love. *We love because he first loved us*" (1 John 4:18,19). In response to such love a child need never be on guard. The warmth and trust so evident sets each one free to *love back* without ever a fear of being pushed away or being misunderstood.

The most sacred trust of the home is to train the capacity for love so that every child can come to know a relationship with God as the heavenly Father so that he can say in truth: "Our *Father* who art in heaven."

Homework for Parents and Teachers—

- How is your own life interpretation of love?
- Are you more concerned about others or yourself?

- Do your children know consistency in their relationship to you?
- For one week watch the look on your child's face when you are displeased with him. Study its meaning.
- Can you discipline your child without breaking a close relationship?
- What does your child learn about forgiveness from you?
- Does your relationship with your child give you freedom and ease in explaining the love of God so the child can understand what you are talking about?

Chapter 7
Imagination for Faith

"Though you have not seen him, you love him; and even though you do not see him now, you believe in him and are filled with an inexpressible and glorious joy, for you are receiving the goal of your faith, the salvation of your souls" (1 Peter 1:8,9).

A mother had just opened the door to the visiting preacher, a three-hundred-pound one! The big preacher looked around for the strongest chair and then sat down on it. Three-year-old Jimmy let out a piercing shriek: "That big man sat down on Peter," he cried. The obliging preacher vacated the chair in favor of "Peter," Jimmy's imaginary playmate.

A child who dreams up "Peter" has plenty of capacity in his imagination for a God whom he cannot see. The only difference is that Jimmy made up "Peter" and the unseen God made Jimmy—with such a capacity to dream up "Peter"! The real problem for a child is not his possible anthropomorphic ideas of God: Father Time style, or any other style. (In fact, these mortal ideas of God he most probably derived from solicitous adults who thought a child could not *see* with his imagination.) The serious problem for a child is not his capacity for imagination, but the ability to distinguish between what is *real* in his imaginings and what is *not real*. He must learn to build a wall between *fact* and *fancy* in his imagination and he must learn to keep each in its own area.

This does not mean that he will learn only the *facts* of the unseen; he should also develop the *fancy* of the unseen. He needs only to know the *difference* between the *fact* and the *fancy* of the world of his imagination. How many poets and artists have been dwarfed because some well-meaning but inept adult labeled him a liar when the child's imagination began to take those delightful flights! This child does not need labeling, he needs encouragement and discernment in the use of his imagination.

Consider the little boy who reported a tiger in the garden. His mother said, "Show me." He took her into the garden where they met tabby cat on the path! The little fellow acted chagrined. His mother looked at him and said, "Son, you'd better go to your room and ask God about your story." After some minutes he returned and reported, "God said He thought it was a tiger at first, too." Mother let herself in for that one! But the little fellow knew the difference, and he knew that his mother knew, and he knew that she knew he knew. A sense of humor is more valuable than a scolding in building this wall in the imagination between fact and fancy. Only those with enough imagination to retain and operate a sense of humor can truly guide a child in the path of truth.

One mother started a game with her little girl the instant the child began imagining stories. With a twinkle in the eye she would ask, "Is this a *really true* story or a *makeup* story?" They had lots of fun together as they built on the makeup story and compared it with the real one. Sometimes the questions to lead the child to discernment were: "How do you wish it had been?" or "What really happened?"

The most successful stories we had in our family story hour when we lived in India were of a "certain family" (ours) and of the things that happened that very day, or of the way they should have happened. Everyone always kept a straight face, but all eyes twinkled. Once I told this story, knowing one son would catch on: "Do you know what? Today the popcorn man came to school at recess. The one little American boy in the school was sorry for all the Indian children who had no money to buy popcorn. They looked hungry, too. So the American boy ran to his home nearby and got all the money in his purse, but it wasn't enough. He emptied his mother's purse, too, and went back to school and passed the money around. The teacher saw that some of the children had big coins to spend and she knew they would never have that much money from home to use on popcorn, so she came to the American boy's mother with the rupees." My son was listening very intently to the story. Here he suddenly interrupted me to say, "That little boy should have asked his mother before he used her money!" What more can a mother ask than that her children learn their lessons the least painful way?

Another evening the story was: "Do you know what I saw today?

Two boys were playing in our front yard under the big banyan tree. All of a sudden they began to quarrel and they kept it up until they hurt each other. When they realized what they were doing they were sorry and they were soon playing happily together again. Do you know why boys feel like fighting sometimes? (wide-eyed looks) Whenever we get angry something called adrenaline gets into our blood and makes us feel like fighting; or it gives us extra energy for running if we meet a tiger out in the jungle. If you will run around the house when you get angry you will use the adrenaline that way and then you won't feel like fighting each other." The next day at play they got angry again. I saw them look at each other quizzically, then suddenly they raced around the house. When they got back to the banyan tree I heard them laugh and shout together, "It works!" I was even more interested than they were in watching it work.

Christmas is the season of the year dearest to a child. It is a time of *real* stories that stretch the imagination of an adult and *make up* stories that delight the heart of a child. All the stories seem real to the child. But if the child knows from the beginning that part of the Santa Claus story is a "make-up" story, he will never have to worry about how Santa can get down a city "chimney" that has no flue.

One of the December delights of every child used to be Dr. Clement Clark Moore's story of *A Visit From St. Nicholas*. Dr. Moore was a writer of scholarly theological books. He was also a devoted father. The story is told that he wrote the St. Nicholas story to entertain his sick child; then he hid the story, but long afterward someone found it. Now all the children of the world can enter into the joy of the imagination of this kind father in his happy story of the jolly old fellow with his reindeer and sleigh.

No child should ever be told anything as a fact that must be unlearned later. He can get great enjoyment out of the Santa Claus story, but the story of the baby Jesus is a *real* story that is basic to all his later experience with God. If the child is led to believe that the unseen Santa Claus is real, he will have difficulty later in believing the reality of the unseen Lord Jesus. He should know the difference from the beginning. He can stretch his imagination all he likes to add to the Santa Claus story, as Dr. Moore did, but his imagination will be enlarged indeed as he learns to know the living Lord who is more real than the things we can touch with our hands.

There has been understandable concern through the years about much that passes as Christmas celebration. On May 11, 1659, the General Court of Massachusetts Bay outlawed Christmas, adding ". . . how could good Christians condone the pagan origin of Christmas. Did not such a holiday encourage excess in eating and drinking?" This was law for a number of years. My own father and many other devout people still felt the same way when I was a child. But we children felt cheated: we had no Santa Claus stories, no Christmas tree or anything else my father called "pagan." I did not know what "pagan" meant, but I thought all the Christmas decorations, stories, and rituals that my little friends had were lovely. I didn't see how any of these things could spoil the baby Jesus story. I know now, with due respect to my father, that our problem at Christmas is not too much imagination, but rather not enough of it. Only God-directed imagination gives the capacity to have fun and be serious at the same time.

Today it is the commercialism of Christmas and other religious holidays that gives concern to the faithful. Too much of this concern is negative and seasonal only. It is futile to wait until the "season" begins to fight the commercialism. Retail business began its plans for next year as soon as last Christmas season was over. The merchants do not ask whether anything is religious or secular, they are pushed to compete with last year's sales. It accomplishes little to compete with their commercialism, but we can *outwit* it.

A new understanding of Christmas and all its customs came to me one afternoon as my sister and I sat in the Art Institute in Chicago listening to Dr. Watson's lecture on Christmas around the world. It was December 8, 1941, the day after Pearl Harbor and the day the United States declared war on Japan and Germany. But the horror of those facts seemed irrelevant as we listened to the wonderful story of God's love gift to the world and all the ways of celebrating this great gift. Dr. Watson said God's love gift to the world was so great that wherever the story was told it was like a love magnet: it drew to itself in every land the stories, legends and customs that were of love and good will. St. Nicholas, the good bishop of Myra in Turkey, was drawn into the celebration because of his love for children and his anonymous giving to the poor that had already become a legend. When Dr. Watson talked about family customs connected with Christmas, he said they came mostly "from those lovely German people." We were at war with Germany, but the spirit of Christmas prevailed!

Imagination is the bridge to the understanding of others. A child cannot be "social" until his imagination develops. When he can imagine enough so that he can enter into the feeling of another person and is able to identify with him, then he is ready to know more of the love of God that is always an understanding love. It is an important day in a child's spiritual development when he says to his mother with understanding concern, "Mummy, are you tired? Let me help you." It is an important day in a mother's life also when her child can use his imagination to enter into her feelings. From this day a new sense of fellowship is possible between mother and child.

This ability to think from the standpoint of another person is tested in a child most of all when a new baby comes, especially if the first child is less than three years of age. A child's imagination is not free to develop in a healthy manner if he has reason to feel neglected or forgotten. If he is permitted to imagine that the baby comes between him and his parents he will not be able to enter into a loving relationship with the new baby. If he was ever rocked in the old rocking chair, he needs it more than ever now. He must be helped to learn that he, with his parents, make up the loving family to which the new baby has come.

Imagination is also the bridge into the future. If it is a healthy imagination it is called *faith.* Expectancy is the handrail on this bridge. A mother can use this joy of expectancy to prepare her child *before* the baby comes. A new baby was coming to three-year-old Becky's house. Becky's mother is an artist as well as a wise mother. She wrote and illustrated a cartoon story just for Becky. This was Becky's most precious book. In it were pictures of Daddy and Mother and Becky getting ready for the new baby. There was a picture of a new bed for Becky and of her old bed put aside for the new baby. There were pictures of Mother going to the hospital and of the home in which Becky would stay while Mother was gone. There were pictures of Mother coming home from the hospital with the new baby and of Becky's share in welcoming him and helping to care for him. This story was read to Becky every day for weeks before the baby came until she knew it all by heart. Then one morning Becky woke up in the neighbor's house! She was so excited she could hardly wait until her new brother came home with Mother. When David came home for the first time, Becky was really ready for him.

As a child's imagination grows enough to think into the future he needs heroes. This need increases as the child's experience grows outside the home. The home is not a place in which to pen up a child, but a place to prepare him for larger social relationships. He must have a lodestar to help keep him in balance when outside pressures of all kinds squeeze in on him. His own school group or his neighborhood group will sometimes seem to be a stronger influence on him than his family. This may bring despair to his parents at times, but the group consciousness and the group loyalty are part of his needed adjustment to a larger social life. The only concern is that he not be a tool of the group, but that he be able to maintain his own integrity.

If the boy already has a hero of high ideals he will be able to gauge his response to the group pressures without undue inner conflict or embarrassment. It is fortunate that the "gang" age and the "hero worshiping age" come at the same time. But if the hero is just like the gang and neither is desirable, the boy is headed for trouble.

Dr. E. Preston Sharp of Philadelphia Youth Center was interviewed by Dave Garroway on the *Today* show April 7, 1958, concerning America's delinquency problems. He said that when the *hero adult* has no more honor than the crowd, the youth in the gang is lost, because he has no balance for the power of the gang on him. Thank God for the youth who do know enough about great heroes who have given their lives in service to mankind. When John Glenn's name was added to the youth's roster of heroes, he brought heroes back into fashion, including the "old fashioned virtues." Fortunate is the boy whose father has earned the privilege of being his son's hero. When a boy has Jesus for a hero he is the most fortunate of all.

The "make-believe" world of a little child is his real world. For a preschool child *play* is his *work,* his whole life. Whatever has any meaning for him becomes a part of his play. Adults forget this some-times because for them play is release from work. If church means anything to a child he will play at preaching and praying. Recently on a Roanoke TV program a mother told of her surprise when her little boy came from the kitchen with a tray of small glasses of *grape juice* and a plate of *small pieces of bread* to serve her guests. He said, "Let's have a church party." This meant that he was so impressed by the commun-ion service, he had to enact it at home.

The ingenuity of a child's imagination at play usually exceeds that of an adult's. Perhaps you've heard the story of the new music teacher who asked the children to act out a song about flowers. Little Johnnie dropped to the floor half way through the song. The teacher chided him sternly: "Get up at once! You are supposed to be a flower. You must have imagination. Now use it!" Johnnie answered, "But I am a flower. My stem broke!" Actually he was more true to life than his teacher.

Play is the schoolroom where the child learns his important lessons for life. If a mother yells at a noisy child to be quiet, he may be cowed into silence but he won't learn anything about the value of silence. If she *plays* silence with him he will find out about a quietness of soul that is imporaant to a child as well as to his mother. He can "play silence" long before he can enjoy taking orders to be silent. Play is the child's means of discovery, of communication and of expression.

Since play *is* the schoolroom for learning life values, we must see play as much more than something to keep children busy while their parents are otherwise occupied. The little girl with her make-believe housekeeping is learning to enjoy the responsibilities that will come to her later. The little girl with her family of dolls is learning to give loving care. If she has dolls of different nations and races she will feel at home with these people, no matter how different they are, whenever she meets them. The little boy with his engines and cars and tools is learn-ing to be a part of a man's world. He enjoys what he learns while he plays. If his greatest joy is in "shooting people" with a gun he is not being trained for a world where "swords will be made into plow-shares." It is one thing for a child to play war when everyone is talking about war, but it is another matter entirely to let it happen from hours of watching TV gunplay as a "baby-sitting device."

Parents may also learn from watching their children at play, for the child is imitative as well as imaginative as he plays the part of an adult. Adults can get a good look at their own foibles and inconsistencies as they are acted out by the children at play. Parents especially can learn much as to action and even tone of voice as their children play "mother and father." They can learn even more if they watch their "cherubs" play "husband and wife"!

One of the neglected spheres of training the imagination is in the field of art. A little girl was asked how she draws her pictures. She said, "I get an idea and then I draw a line around it." This kind of art is language to a child. He can "write" this language long before he can write words. Many children have no encouragement to write this "language" because parents and even Sunday school teachers give them only lines to stay inside of for coloring. Of course, these color books give muscle training and leeway for color choice, but they give no opportunity whatever for the language of a child's imagination. To our six-year-old grandson David, it was a real worship experience of joy to draw the Christmas angels. He was sure they could hardly wait to see the baby Jesus, so he drew them "hurrying to find the baby Jesus." This meant so much more to David than to stay within someone else's lines, even though their lines might be more realistic. But then, who knows what angels look like anyway?

Above all, our imaginations need to be trained so we can have real faith. Marcus Aurelius said, "Our lives are dyed the color of our imaginations." *Faith is trained imagination that has learned to know fact from fancy and is master of both.* "Faith is being sure of what we hope for, and certain of what we do not see" (Heb. 11:1). This faith is a *shield* that not only protects one from evil, but makes it possible to "extinguish all the flaming arrows of the evil one" (Eph. 6:16). Trained imagination opens the door to the greatest adventures of life. It opened the door to the space age; more than that, it opens the door to the spaceless age. It helps us to know ourselves as the children of God in the midst of a distraught world. This is the faith we want our children to have.

When the imagination is undeveloped, retarded, or in any way diseased, we call it *worry* or *anxiety*. In worry or anxiety, fear is in control, rather than faith. Too many people are like the little boy who came downstairs to tell his mother, "I'm not going to sleep until that figment of my imagination gets out from under my bed!" His mother, if wise, will use every means possible to help her child get rid of his fear of the dark. If she is not afraid of the unknown in her life she will find it easier to lead her child into faith. He will learn more anyway from her own faith than from any words she might use.

Helping a child to conquer fear does not mean that he will become careless or indifferent to danger. There are many dangers a child must be taught to recognize, but in recognizing them he need not be prey to them.

The experience of death in the family brings the greatest test of trained mature imagination. If the loved adults give themselves up to excessive grief a child may find death to be a banging door to a black unknown. In such a case he not only faces whatever personal loss he has but also the insecurity he will feel with the living who also seem lost to him. But even where adults are mature and Christian in the face of death, the experience is still difficult for a child to understand.

It is fortunate if a child's first experience of death is with a pet and not a parent. Our first experience was in the death of five baby rabbits. The mother rabbit was very special to our children. They were grieved when the red ants stung the babies to death. The children conducted a funeral and we saw the five little boxes consigned to the earth.

After some days I noticed a terrible odor in our house. I looked in every corner to find the cause. More days went by and still we had not found the cause of the odor which grew steadily worse. Then one day when I was teaching my son, Merrill, at his little table, I saw some fat worms crawling out of some boxes stacked on the corner of the table. Right there under my nose all the time was the cause of the odor. Merrill had dug up the boxes of dead rabbits, hoping for a resurrection! Needless to say, we had to have another burial.

A boy lost a pet horse. His grief was so great, his father wanted to buy him another at once; but his mother thought he should first learn to accept the loss. She was very glad he learned this lesson for not long after this he lost his father by death. His daddy could not be replaced. The loss of the horse helped prepare him for this greater loss because of his mother's wisdom and faith in both experiences.

The superintendent of the primary department of a large Sunday school in Chicago was greatly loved by all the children. She had such a creative gift with children that she never had discipline problems. One September day she became very ill. The children all prayed for her to get well. They wanted her back with them. They thought God would answer their prayer for her to get well, but just before Christmas she died. It fell to the Christian education director of the church to tell the children the next Sunday that Miss Beulah was gone. He told me that he spent more time on that explanation for the children than he ever did on any sermon. He had to face a child's loss of a loved one, but even more critical, a child's faith in a God of love who always hears the prayers of His children. After he made his explanation a boy raised his hand and said, "I know what you mean. Sometimes I go visiting with my parents in the evening. They stay so long I fall asleep. They bring me home, undress me and put me to bed while I am still asleep. The next morning when I wake up, I'm at home. That's what happened to Miss Beulah. She woke up at home with God." So the children did understand what he tried to tell them. Death, to a Christian, is only a final opening incident and not an interruption in the life with God.

So "faith is being sure of what we hope for, and certain of what we do not see."

Faith is a gift of God's grace. Those with trained imaginations find it much easier to receive this gift of faith.

Homework for Parents and Teachers—

- A five-year-old little Baptist girl had a Catholic friend. When she found how different the Catholic girl was, she did not want her to feel different, so she said to her, "I understand: I was a Catholic before I was a Baptist!" If you were her mother, how would you nurture her good motive and still help her speak "the truth"?
- Classify your child's make-up stories: are they for joy or from some fear?
- Do you know the difference between credulity and faith?

Chapter 8
Choice for Commitment

A young girl in Ohio asked, "Why doesn't God make me be good?" In the very creation God limited Himself by giving man the right and responsibility of choice. To this day He has never forced anyone to be good. He never makes our decisions for us. He planned for us to do that. He gave us enough freedom to make those choices. He does not make us follow Him, but He revealed Himself as Love in Jesus Christ and this love makes us *want* to follow Him. "For Christ's love compels us, because we are convinced. . . He died for all, that those who live should no longer live for themselves but for him who died for them and was raised" (2 Cor. 5:14,15). This love draws us to Him so that we can choose Him and give our lives to Him without fear. But this choosing we must do ourselves.

The Lord says, "Come unto Me," but He does not *come* for us. We have to do our *coming* for ourselves. He wants *response* and *obedience* from us, but He does not do our *responding* or our *obeying* for us. We must do our own.

It is the *capacity* for coming, for responding, for obeying that must be trained "before grace" so that a person can be ready to receive grace. Most of the spiritual problems that adults have are from their inadequately trained capacity to receive and hold what God gives them. People come with tiny or leaky cups to receive God's blessing. God wants to use His great measure in giving to us: "But to each one of us grace has been given as Christ apportioned it . . . . until we all reach unity in the faith and in the knowledge of the Son of God and become mature, attaining to the whole measure of the fullness of Christ. Then we will be no longer infants . . . . instead, speaking the truth in love, we will in all things grow up into him who is the Head, that is, Christ" (Eph. 4:7–15). So even "after grace" the *increasing* of the capacity is necessary. "Before grace" it is growing *toward* Christ. "After grace" it is growing *in* Christ.

If Christianity were merely subscribing to a set of doctrines or beliefs, then a good memory would be the capacity most essential for the acceptance of God's offer of salvation. If Christianity were merely doing certain commanded rituals and performing certain deeds then mere obedience would be enough. But being a child of God is more than committing the truths of God to memory. It is more than blindly obeying certain rituals or doing a number of good deeds. The religion that Jesus revealed by His life and teaching requires the *giving* of one's *whole life* to God in a new personal relationship. Dependence on ritual performance and good deeds can become a religious substitute and can actually separate one from God if the *whole life* is not given to Him.

Mere obedience is no guarantee of character. The *reason* for the obedience is the determining factor. This capacity for choice in obedience must develop and grow even after one is a Christian. Some of the early Christians were slow in learning this lesson. They were still in the nursery when it was time for them to be teachers: "But solid food is for the mature, *who by constant use have trained themselves to distinguish good from evil*" (Heb. 5:14).

It is only when the "outward must" becomes the "inward ought" that any child begins to grow up. If a parent or teacher is satisfied with mere outward obedience after a child has some understanding of his actions, then that parent or teacher is shortchanging the child. A parent or teacher is successful only as a child learns to take over the responsibility for his own choices. I remember the parents who were so proud of their thirteen-year-old daughter. "She is such an obedient girl, she always does what pleases us." They were blind. She told others she was waiting for the day when she could do as *she* pleased. That day came and she broke their hearts. They could not understand it. "She was such a 'good' girl." They didn't see that she had never developed any inner strength, that she had no discernment about right and wrong, that she only obeyed. When those in authority over her changed she obeyed just as easily.

The immature person obeys blindly as the easiest way out, or rebels merely to defy authority. The maturing person learns to choose. This is an old story. In fact, it is the Old Testament story! The people were so slow to learn, they were called stiffnecked and rebellious. Still God did not force men to be good.

God tried one more plan. He sent His Son into the world to live among men as a man. Love became incarnate, even to the final suffering from men who refused to see Him as God. But in the cross, something new had been added, the revealed love of God brought a different kind of compulsion: *the love of Christ that impels us.* This love does not force men to come to God, it makes them *want to* come to Him. It reaches for the capacity in man created to *respond* to God. It melts away rebellion. It eliminates all sense of servitude. It makes impossible the passivity that retards growth, and it sets the individual free to make the right choice for life.

Martin Buber said man does not *discover* God, he *responds* to Him. Little children in their outreach to life are set for this response to life and to God. They are on the way if they are not caused to stumble. This is why Jesus said the adult must become like a child, and why it is so terrible to make one of these little ones to stumble. To hurt the capacity for response in a child is to limit his chance to become a child of God. For an adult to lose this childlike ability to respond means that he closes the door of his life to God.

The problem of "good character" is still with us. The perennial question haunts us more than ever: How does character develop? The Christian has failed in his answer when he fails to distinguish between what man can do for himself and what he cannot do. Some good people try to do God's part without even trying to do their own part. They lazily expect the grace of God to pick them up and make them wonderful people when they don't even accept the disciplines of obedience to God's love. To say the least such people are a nuisance to have around the house. This lazy Christian is loveless and he hides behind the *doctrine* of grace. But Jesus said, "All men will know that you are my disciples if you love one another" (John 13:35).

Suppose I don't love someone with whom I have to live. We say we cannot help it that love is not in our hearts. That is a fact. We cannot *make* ourselves love. But there is something we can do. We can seek to understand the person we do not love. We can consider what Jesus must think of him. We can seek to do him some kindness. Then the miracle begins to happen. We have given God the chance He waited for, *to give us His love.* His love is always a gift of grace, but it is never ours until we receive it and are willing to act on it.

When we learn to distinguish between God's part and our part in cooperating with Him we will have learned some of the greatest secrets of Christian education. We cannot do it all, but neither can God, because He has given us the power to choose.

Children do not grow into character by osmosis as was hoped a generation ago. To merely provide a good environment and expect a child to be molded automatically into the desired image proved to be a false conclusion. Some children with "unfortunate environments" turned out very well. In fact, they seemed stronger for the difficulties they had to overcome. And an increasing number of children out of the "best environments" have turned out to be delinquent.

The environment was important, of course, but the *attitude toward the environment* proved to be the deciding factor. Character results are according to the reaction of each child to his environment. If he is passive he is molded by his environment. If he is active in his choice he can use his environment as a stepping stone. In any case the environment need not be a hindrance.

The definition for environment was also at fault. When the environment was thought of in terms of things, comforts, readymade opportunities, the "rights of the individual," children grew up waiting for life to make their choices for them. Life does not do this. *Blaming* life, the family, or anyone does not solve anyone's problem. *A child's real environment is in his relationships.* If his relationships are what they ought to be in a family he can withstand almost any physical environment.

Peter and Jennifer were friends of our children when we lived in India. During the war they were sent to relatives in England to go to school. When the bombs began to fall they were sent with other children from London out into the beautiful countryside where they had good food, sunshine, and safety. Later these same children were brought back to the dangerous life in London with their relatives. They were found to have more security with their loved ones in the midst of danger than they had in the safety of the beautiful country. The real environment that counts is in the child's *relationships*.

A little baby does develop at first by "absorption." He is a helpless little fellow so he cannot do anything but receive. But he is unconsciously learning from those who love him. His ethical values are forming as he learns to trust his parents. As he grows he learns kindness, love, justice, honesty, consistency, and dependability from them if they are good parents to him. Later on when he learns the words for these qualities he will already be familiar with their meanings.

As the little one grows in responsiveness to those who love him he learns to love back, and he begins to imitate their ways because he wants to be like them. At this age the learning process is by imitation. He cannot really learn gracious ways unless he sees them in the family relationships. He cannot learn table manners unless he sees them. At this age he will also learn to pray and worship according to what he sees. He will learn courage or anxiety according to what his parents are in their inner lives. Parents should now appreciate the fact that this little fellow is a real mirror of their lives. Before they deal too harshly with him for untoward behavior they should first look to themselves to see if he is imitating them. Perhaps *they* need the discipline.

As a child continues to grow he begins to find out, as he should, that he is a person in his own right, an individual separate from those he loves. He is fortunate if he already has the security of a consistent relationship with his own family. The outreach toward life and growth in him will have to experiment with this developing consciousness of freedom as a separate individual. So he passes from the dependence of early childhood so dear to his loved ones, to the uninhibited age of two, three, or even four and five. Now he will feel impelled to say no on every possible occasion. This is his lesson assignment for this age. The responsibility of his parents is to help him to say no at the proper times and not to let him become merely negative. But how can he learn to choose if he doesn't know how to say no as well as yes?

The little fellow may fail in this important lesson if his parents are frustrated or angered by his sudden uncooperativeness. Actually this turn of events is not a vote *against* mother, it is a vote *for* the emerging self-consciousness of the little man. If he feels ''attacked'' or disrespected he will be bound to fire back and he will be thrown into conflict with the very adults whom he loves the most. If he loses the security of the relationship he had before, he will fail to find the self he was unconsciously seeking. His parents need to know what is in process in his growing life.

If his parents fail him, the lesson of this period will turn from a discovery of self to a fight for individuation. Many people, through such misunderstanding, have never grown beyond this negative period. They feel bound to reject anything anyone else suggests. The no that should have developed into an alternative for a yes takes over the whole field. By the adolescent years rebellion against family and society may lead to real delinquency. If delinquency is by-passed the adult years may be complicated by a helpless competitive spirit. Some parents can't help or understand their children because they haven't found themselves yet. If you are such a bewildered parent look at the signs of your immaturity. Do you feel impelled to do the opposite if your mate makes a suggestion to you? Someone said an efficiency expert is a person paid a high salary to do what is called nagging if a wife does it. Or if it is your mate who is helplessly negative are you mature enough to give him space to find himself as he evidently did not do when he was four? At any age the process seems to be the same. Recognize the merely negative attitude for what it is, an unlearned four-year-old lesson!

When a child is first impelled to say no he must also learn to say yes. For now he is at the beginning of the road that parts into two ways and he must learn to choose which way he will go. If he does not learn to say "yes" also he will be a slave to his own emotional reactions and will not be free to make any choice. The things that he should say yes to must be very clear to him or he will not be able to choose. This is why he needs parents who are mature enough to differentiate the various choices.

The greatest danger in *prejudice* in the hearts of people is that one area of the mind is closed to thinking. The darkness of fear makes choice of action impossible. This prejudice may concern difference in people, difference in religion, difference in politics. But it is prejudice, nevertheless, as long as we fear to look at both sides. Perhaps we are afraid to look at both sides sometimes because we don't have our own securities established.

A Virginia schoolteacher, some years ago, found such an opportunity for enlightenment. Children love the light. They enjoy "catching on" to a new situation. She announced to her one-room school that a family of migrants had moved into the community and five new children would be coming to school. A hand went up, "My grandma says they are poor white trash and not our kind of people." Others felt the same way. So the teacher told the story of a migrant family: they had to move so often on account of the father's work. The children had to change school so often; sometimes they were not welcomed and so it was hard to find friends.

What would her children do? To her joy, the next day the new children were given a great welcome. At noon her pupils had shared so much of their lunches that the desks of the new children were piled with food. By the end of the year several of the new children were star pupils. This was the first chance they had had to have real friends. God extends His love to others through those who already know Him. In the light of His love and understanding the darkness of all fear and prejudice can be dispelled.

Conflicts between parents and children are ancient history. It is reported that Socrates four centuries before Christ complained:

> Children now love luxury, they have bad manners, contempt for authority, they show disrespect for elders and love to chatter in place of exercise. Children are now tyrants not slaves of the household. They no longer rise when an elder enters the room, they contradict their parents, chatter before company, gobble up the food at the table, cross their legs, and tyrannize their teachers.

We have advanced in one matter in our day, the alternative is no longer between tyranny and slavery so far as the children are concerned. But some mothers wonder now and then if that is the only choice the parents have! It has been rumored around the world that American children "rule the roost." It is more than fifty years since the child as a real person was rediscovered. As followers of Jesus we should never have lost sight of the tremendous importance of the childhood years. With the realization of the great neglect of understanding childhood many went too far in featuring children and their wishes. The child was too often permitted to do whatever he pleased for fear of ruining his budding personality. This was called "permissiveness." The child was permitted to find his own way of doing. Adults forgot that they have an advantage and a responsibility from their experience. The fruits of the years of too much permissiveness are upon us and a great disillusionment has hit many who have to do with children.

The basic emphasis on permissiveness was good. It came out of the disillusionment about the effects on a child of autocratic authoritarianism. The question is not concerning tyranny or enslavement or sheer obedience as such. The leading thinkers of our day are pushing through the fog to find the balance between *authority* and *permissiveness*. So much has been learned about the ways of a child and the manner of his growth that the way should soon be clear to help a child to grow to his best fulfillment. This will be as good for the parents as for the children.

The only legitimate authority an adult has is in his responsibility to train children to make their own decisions. Parents who are angry and feel affronted or defied when their children try to think for themselves are failing in the authority invested in them as parents. Such shortsighted parents don't want children, they want puppets. They unwittingly exploit the children for their own prestige and satisfaction. The greatest adventure a parent can experience is to search for and discover each child's own individuality and to help him grow in his own way, at his own speed, to his own greatest fulfillment.

The balance between authority and permissiveness can be found only as obedience is required for truth's sake and not demanded in the name of parental authority or of superior age. Parents with their larger experience may expect their children to join them in a mutual allegiance to the greater authority of truth in the name of God. Such a joint obedience to truth should eliminate much of the rebellion children feel today toward their parents and teachers. Humbly facing truth together should eliminate the competitiveness between the age groups. In such an experience parents will even be free to confess their own failures without losing the respect of their children, or without losing their own dignity. They will also set an example for the children to confess their failures without feeling undue condemnation.

Parents who let their children make choices as they are able find another difficulty that may be even harder. They must learn to let their children bear the consequences of any wrong choices they might make. Louise was careful in spending her allowance, but Adele, two years older, was a spendthrift. It was hard for their mother to see Adele having to go without some pleasure which Louise could afford because of her thrift, but the mother wisely let Adele learn her lesson.

However, sometimes children are permitted to make choices for which they are not prepared. One young woman of twenty-five told me that for years she found it hard to forgive her parents for permitting her to make a choice at thirteen which she did not know enough to make. Her parents were returning to the mission field for another seven years after a long furlough. They let her decide whether she would go with them or stay in America. She did not want to leave her friends or her school and she could not know what seven adolescent years without her parents would mean. She decided to stay in America. The loneliness and anxieties of those years before airmail service were too much for one so young. She was given the responsibility of choosing beyond her experience.

Children often give a clue as to what they can do. Little Johnnie fell down the porch steps. He cried, but when his granddaddy started to pick him up he said with dignity, "I can pick myself up." When I was a child we knelt down on our knees for prayer in family worship. Four-year-old Esther forgot her prayer. From across the room I suggested the possible next words. The first thing I knew I received a kick in the rear. Esther said, "I can say it myself." Then she returned to kneel by her chair, to finish her prayer herself!

As long as a child is permitted to make choices in the area where he can make a responsible choice he is in his *area of free choice,* as Dr. Fritz Kunkel called it. The child would be bewildered by too large a selection to choose from (like adults in a modern cafeteria), but he can practice in choosing between beets and spinach, peaches or pears. Of course, if he has the choice between pie and cake he would choose both! A six-year-old has no choice about going to school or staying at home when he is well, but he can choose which school clothes he will wear.

The child who has learned by practice to choose the right from the wrong is well prepared for the end of childhood's days of dependence and for the opening world of adolescence where he will have to make choices whether he is prepared or not.

The greatest choice in life is the choice to give one's life to God. The next most important choice is a life companion. The third great choice is for vocation. All three of these choices are frequently made before adolescence is completed. Those untrained for choosing often ignore the first important choice and then blunder into the other two. Fortunate is the youth who knows and wants to choose God in the days when he feels the life pressure for personal independence. With God he will learn then how to grow in preparedness for the other great choices of life.

Homework for Parents and Teachers—

- How many things do you do for your children that they could do for themselves?
- What responsibilities of choice do your children have?
- Are they learning to be dependable?
- Do your children rebel often? Why?
- For a week make a list of success and failures in these areas.

Chapter 9
Discipline for Responsibility of Choice

Many Christians do not have much difficulty in making the right choices: their difficulty is in maintaining the discipline of a good choice. The power of the Spirit that makes new life possible, we will consider later; but here we consider a training in responsibility that creates a *capacity* in which the Spirit can operate. God does not do for us what we should do for ourselves. Adults need always to remember that the responsibility of choice must eventually be transferred to the child. To have the child accept this moral responsibility is the goal of our training.

For two weeks I had the privilege of helping to care for Danny, an entrancing four-year-old. He had been an unusually cooperative child until his world turned topsy turvy: his father died, his home was changed, and now his mother was ill. Most of the time he was his old sweet self, but by streaks he would suddenly come through the house like a cyclone, knocking down everything en route. His loved ones understood his insecurity; they did their best, but the tirades continued sporadically.

I felt sure the little fellow would have more security if behavior boundaries were set, and perhaps I had a better chance to set them since I was the unknown quantity in the household, even though he knew me well. So the first time I was the lone audience for a "cyclone" I quietly walked up to him, took hold of his arms firmly and looked him steadily in the eyes. He looked back expecting me to do something *to* him: but I kept the steady hold on his arms and said, "Danny, when little boys act that way I hold them like this until they get quiet inside." He did not struggle at all. After thinking for a moment he said, "You can let go now. I won't do it again." I said, "That's fine," and let go. The next day he had to find out if I was consistent, so he started on a rampage again, with one eye on me. I walked slowly toward him as I had done the day before. Before I reached him, he suddenly grabbed his arms himself and said, "You don't have to hold me. *I can hold myself.*" And he did hold himself from then on. This is, indeed, the goal: that each child learn to hold himself.

Discipline has a very definite relationship to the responsibility of choice when we consider its real meaning. Its general negative connotation is a misrepresentation of its real meaning. The fact that *discipline* and *disciple* come from the same root word is suggestive of the positive meaning of discipline. Anyone can punish a child but only those who can make disciples of the children can truly discipline them. When we see discipline as a positive directive in life we no longer do something *to* a child but we do something *for* him or *with* him so that he will want to change for the better. The transfer from the *outward must,* so necessary in infancy, to the *inward ought* as the child grows in understanding, then becomes possible. Each occasion for constructive discipline is only another lesson in a lifelong process of learning under the guidance of parents and of God.

When the Hebrew Christians were restive under persecution they were told: "My son, do not make light of the Lord's discipline, and do not lose heart when he rebukes you, because the Lord disciplines those he loves, and he punishes everyone he accepts as a son. Endure hardship as discipline; God is treating you as sons. For what son is not disciplined by his father? If you are not disciplined (and everyone undergoes discipline), then you are illegitimate children and not true sons. . . . No discipline seems pleasant at the time, but painful. Later on, however, it produces a harvest of righteousness and peace for those who have been trained by it" (Heb. 12:5–11).

Even Jesus learned obedience: "Although he was a son, he learned obedience from what he suffered and, once made perfect, He became the source of eternal salvation for all who obey him" (Heb. 5:8,9).

The obedience of a child grows in moral and spiritual value only as he learns to take over for himself the development of his own inner strength. When an adult realizes that he is working and watching for this inner takeover of responsibility for action, discipline takes on a new dimension. Most conscientious parents recognize the importance of this transfer of moral responsibility from parent to child, but too often they fail to realize that the path to that goal is made up of *seemingly insignificant incidents* day by day.

One day I rode home on the upper deck of a double-decker bus. A man with his three-year-old son sat in front of me. The father waited until the bus stopped at his corner to start down the steep steps. Hastily he started to pick up his son to carry him down the steps. I never saw such insulted dignity. With firmness the little fellow said, "No, Daddy, I walk." The father called down to the driver to wait, and the little fellow went down those steps on his own feet with all the dignity a three-year-old could muster. He was quite willing, however, to take his father's hand. This father did well to respect his son's desire to do what he could.

A child has a real growing joy in doing whatever he is able to do. Another three-year-old expressed this joy in the refrain "all by my lone" whenever she did something all by herself. It was, "When I wake up in the morning I can get out of my bed all by my lone," and, "I can wash my hands and my face and brush my teeth all by my lone." Her progress was joy to her and poetry to her parents.

When we came back to America from India our daughter was a junior in high school. America was really a foreign land to our children for they had grown up in India. They had many adjustments to make in the transfer from their beautiful mountain school to a crowded city school. I did not want them to have an added self-consciousness because of difference in clothes, but a missionary's budget is not like India rubber. Lois's best friend was a beautiful Greek girl who had lovely American clothes. It was hard for me to know what Lois needed and what she merely wanted. One day she came home from school and said excitedly: "I have to have a new dress by Friday night." I suggested that she go to the nearby store to buy a pattern for material we already had on hand. She answered, "Oh, Mother, let's let it go. I don't have time to go to the store." The secret I needed was out: give daughter the responsibility of the first step toward answering her request. If it is a *want* and not a *need* she will drop the matter. This cooperative method saved us many times from mother-daughter misunderstandings. A sharing of responsibility leads to a deeper fellowship.

Obedience to early necessary constraint and direction needs to grow into a cooperative experience. Often we do not know how far children have progressed in their ability to cooperate until we watch them at play. On the playground they are very particular about obeying rules, about taking turns and about being fair. There they take moral responsibility for what they consider to be "right" or "wrong." Whatever ability for judgment they have on the playground should have full opportunity for expression off the playground. Too many times, a child is fair, considerate, and brave on the playground, but in his mother's kitchen he is a different child—a big baby who wants his own way! He would be happier and mother would have less frustration if she learned what his real ability for sharing responsibility is.

Children are usually much more advanced in moral judgment than we give them credit for. Little Debbie came downstairs and announced to her mother: "I need to be spanked." She had done something that displeased her mother and now she wanted the issue settled so she could forget it! Of course, "wrong" at first means *displeasing parents*. And the request for punishment is the desire for forgiveness or restored relationship. Parents carry the responsibility of training a child's conscience by the very act of their displeasures as well as by those things which please them in their children. A child must know that table manners are not as serious an issue as unkindness to little brother, even though they must learn both.

As a child grows in responsibility of judgment the "inner voice" that passes judgment for good or ill can just as easily be considered the voice of God. This is not hard for a child. Perhaps this is the easiest way for parents to find how much a child has grown in his responsible thinking. One day in seminary class I told my students about four-year-old Beth in India. She had cut the table cloth, the curtains, and her hair with her new kindergarten scissors. Then she waited to be spanked! Her mother had just been reading about the importance of being quiet before God, so she decided to try it on Beth. She suggested that they be real quiet before God and see what He would say to them. After some minutes mother asked Beth if she heard anything. Beth answered, "Yes, Jesus told me not to cut the wrong things with my scissors, and that you are to take them away until I learn to cut the right things."

One father in my class was sure this would never work with his children. That evening when he went home he found that his four-year-old Maryann had written all over the inside cover of an expensive new book. He saw that she was waiting for his reproof or punishment, so he decided to try the quiet way also. He suggested to Maryann that they be silent before God, to think about what God would say. Looking to God meant words to her so she started to pray aloud, but her daddy said, "No, this time we will not talk, we will listen." So they listened for awhile. Then he asked if she heard anything. Maryann said, "God told me not to write in books, and to get an eraser and erase what I had scribbled in this one." Helping a child to take his responsibility for his actions as much as he is able to judge, is vital to his moral growth. Also, when a child has a chance to take the responsibility for admitting his own mistakes, the conflict between accusing parent and defensive child is avoided.

A large part of the responsibility of choice is patience, tension capacity, or the ability to put off a minor pleasure of the moment in order to have a greater blessing later on. Little tots do not begin life with this kind of patience. They have to learn it—from parents who have it. A child hears: "Wait to eat, wait to wear a new dress, wait to go out to play!" All he knows is that he wants to do it now. But he must learn to wait. By the time he is adolescent all his future happiness will depend on whether he learns deliberately to forego an immediate, limited satisfaction so that he may reach a fuller, more lasting one later.

Adults who have not learned the responsibilities that go with the ability to choose have a difficult time with "left-over" unlearned lessons. Learning four-year-old lessons at forty is not child's play. One young minister could not get up in the morning. This habit seemed to be the symbol of all his "left-over" lessons. At night he would tell his wife: "Please get me up in the morning, no matter how I act then." She would try, but he would roll over for more sleep. Both were in despair. Finally the victory came with God's help and he felt at last that he had left his childhood to his memories. Even his sermons took on a new quality of faith and assurance!

Passive obedience is not responsible obedience. It is virtue only when it is a *chosen obedience.* This kind of obedience has to be won, it cannot be forced. Only integrity and consistency in parents can hold the respect of the child. Somehow children seem to have an innate sense of justice. When parents respect the child's integrity they win the respect of the child. The child seems to learn that together with his parents he and they obey a truth beyond themselves. When the child feels more responsibility in answering to truth than even to his parents, he is set free to make his own decision and to live by what he has chosen.

Ivan wanted to be a minister, but he was having problems in making and holding to his decision. One day he told about his very religious parents: "My mother was a Sunday school teacher. She wasn't the same on Sunday as during the week. I learned the art of presenting a good and acceptable 'front.' " Of his father he said the repeated demand was: "Do it the way I tell you, even if it is wrong." As a child he thought God was a sort of tyrant who made uncompromising demands beyond any child's reach, who made an assignment sheet with a long list of things he, as a child, had to do to be acceptable to God. It took him years to break away from these childhood fears of God.

When there is *consistent love* in the home, a child obeys his parents without questioning the rightness of their position on any matter; but when he is old enough to have relationships outside the home, he hears other interpretations. When he has great respect for these other people also, he is bound to be perplexed by their difference of view and even of conscience. But if his capacity for responsible decision making is well trained, he will be able to think for himself without being torn between those he loves and other good people.

A high-school girl from a very conservative home asked, "My parents conscientiously believe one way, I conscientiously believe another way. How can I get along with my parents?" She was in the first real steps of doing her own thinking but having difficulty in the relationships involved. Her good parents did not know how important it was for her to learn to think. They wanted her to copy their thoughts. They thought that respect for them as parents meant an unthinking obedience to their desires, even throughout adolescence. The girl found her freedom in understanding her parents and in not rebelling against them, even though she continued to do her own thinking.

Rebellious thinking or action is not responsible thinking or action. It is too negative. However, in the beginning a child's rebellion may be more positive than negative. It may be that he is not resisting authority so much as he is trying to find his own way of thinking and doing. He may be trying to push away a blanket of domination so he can do his own breathing. It is very important for adults to recognize this "rebellion" for what it is. If they do not recognize it as essentially a responsible quality they will turn it into irresponsible rebellion.

Unfortunately there are many people in responsible positions who think of rebellion as being synonymous with independent thinking. The fear of "momism" in the army during the war may have had something to do with the encouragement of rebellion as a cult. "Momism" was immaturity in both "mom" and her son. It had nothing to do with a good home. Some young people have been made to feel self-conscious and even guilty when they wanted to spend vacations at home. But breaking home ties doesn't necessarily imply independent thinking. Home ties should never be broken. The home should be the foundation experience in life. Tearing out foundations is shaky business. *In the beginning the parents hold the strings of the home ties, then they let the children hold the strings.* The strings should always be there, not to bind, but to retain security with freedom.

The child who has obeyed his parents out of fear may continue through life acting out of fear. He will "obey" God because he is afraid of God; he will avoid "sin" only for fear he may be found out; he will join the church for fear of otherwise going to hell; he will live always in fear. He will not know what it means to be the child of a God of love, a love that casts out all fear.

The child who knows only fear and rebellion will also have difficulty in learning to know God who does not *make* anyone follow Him. The rebellious pattern of life is the essence of sin by the prophet's definition: "a stiff-necked and rebellious people." Even a good thing chosen out of rebellion may bring increased conflicts. Some have gone to the mission field to get *away from* parental domination. Even more young people have entered marriage to get away from home. *To get away from* is not reason to go anywhere. God waits—He has been called the Waiting Father—for us to choose Him because we *want* Him.

Autonomy of conscience and responsibility of choice are possible only when the outreach is *toward* truth and the God who is Truth, and not merely *against* the past or *against* sin. Only the youth who has learned to choose, and has learned the discipline of the responsibility of maintaining a choice, will be free to choose God and His way. There must be a disciplined core of purpose, but no hardness from rebellion, if we would have our hearts ready to receive Him.

The apostle Paul said it well: "With eyes wide open to the mercies of God, I beg you, my brothers, as an act of intelligent worship, to give Him your bodies, as a living sacrifice, consecrated to Him and acceptable by Him. Don't let the world around you squeeze you into its mould, but let God remould your minds from within, so that you may prove in practice that the plan of God for you is good, meets all His demands and moves toward the goal of true maturity" (Rom. 12:1, 2 Phillips).

Homework for Parents and Teachers—

- Keep a record for a week of the commands you give your children.
- Are they wise commands and few enough, so that you can see if they are obeyed?
- Have your children learned to carry through with their responsibilities in the home? If not, why not?
- When a spirit of rebellion enters in any family relationships, find the cause.
- What do you do if your children try to think for themselves? Note the occasion, the child's reason, your reaction, the result in the child's life.
- How are you faring in *your* commitments to God?

Chapter 10

Disciplined Mind for Discernment of Truth

A state university teacher told me her religion had nothing to do with her mind; it was for her emotions only. She was somewhat frustrated by the team that had come to her university for religious emphasis week. We did not come on her "days" for religion, we came during the week. She didn't want to *think* her religion, she just wanted to *feel* it. It is a false conception to separate the mind and its "intellectual pursuits" from the emotions and "religious pursuits." The little child is nearer the truth when he sees no distinction between the secular and the sacred. The modern, as well as the biblical approach to the wholeness of personality is against compartmentalizing the person.

In biblical language the heart was not merely the seat of compassion, but was regarded as the source of man's intellectual activities. *Mind* and *heart* were used so much in the same way that one version translates the same word as *mind,* and another as *heart.* He plans in his *heart* (1 Kings 8:48; Isa. 10:7). The laws of God were written in man's *heart* (King James) or *mind* (Modern Language) (1 Kings 3:9). Jesus challenged the scribes, "Why do you argue this way in your *hearts?*" (Mark 2:8).

In biblical language the heart was thought of as the repository and directive center of thought, will, feeling, and conscience. It was the focus of man's inner personal life. So when we give our hearts to God we give Him our all. God gave man the responsibility to learn to think, to learn to think new thoughts. God cannot do anything with lazy minds that are so complacent they cannot respond to Him. He wants to give us His thoughts but we cannot receive them unless we do our part. The early church had trouble with the Christians who were retarded in their growth because they did not use their minds to do their own thinking, their own choosing of God and His way: ". . . you need someone to teach you the elementary truths of God's word all over again. You need milk, not solid food . . . . But solid food is for the mature, who by constant use have trained themselves to distinguish good from evil" (Heb. 5:11–14).

As a child, Jesus Himself "grew in wisdom" (Luke 2:52). Of Himself He later said, "For this reason I was born, and for this I came into the world, to testify to the truth. Everyone on the side of truth listens to me" (John 18:37). Listening to the voice of Jesus is no passive attitude. This means the same as when He said we should hunger and thirst after righteousness. The righteousness, or truth of God, is available to the one who reaches for it. Children are always so eager to learn. In this adults must be childlike. Without an alert mind for listening and learning God cannot teach us His truth.

A healthy, well-cared for child is always alert and alive to the new and the unknown. He never loses his thirst for knowledge or adventure, *unless* he is slapped back until he loses courage. He needs discipline at times, of course, but directing him in his outreach to learn new things will include this discipline, which is a different thing from slapping him down.

This alert outreach of the child shows first in his great *physical activity*. Not a muscle is unused in a baby's daily contortions. By this activity he is learning to control his muscles until he can reach for what he wants and later go where he wants to go. Without guidance and barricades he will pull down the fish bowl, empty bureau drawers, and fall down steps. The barricades must be there to protect him from what he does not understand, but they must also give him enough room for safe investigation of the new world he is discovering. His activity must never be considered a nuisance; it is a necessity for his growth in wisdom and stature. Someone has said that a junior has ninety-nine muscles with which to wiggle and only one with which to keep quiet. Healthy energy is for growing and we must cope with it without irritation.

One mother on a long car trip alone with four children stopped every few hours and had the children run around to get rid of their piled up energy. Then, with quiet entertainment in the car, she did not have to keep scolding them while she kept her eyes on the road. A good Sunday school teacher of little children also knows that "being good" and "sitting still" are not always synonymous terms. She has activities and action songs because God made little children full of activity and He understands about their growing bodies.

Another quality of the alert child that seems to an adult to be a liability rather than an asset is a child's consuming *curiosity*. Curiosity is a child's hunger and thirst for knowledge: without it there is no real education. Therefore it is all-important to keep his curiosity sharp and growing. It is a crime to blunt it, for it is his push to knowledge.

As soon as a child can talk the questions begin. A thousand times he asks, ''What's this?'' Only thoughtless adults will be irritated by this endless questioning. In a family where seeking questions are respected, a child will easily learn more than he will ever learn in any other five years of his life. All of life is new to a child. How else can he learn about his world? Every question he asks is an opportunity for learning as well as an opportunity for strengthening of parent-child relationships. Some parents of adolescents would give anything if their children would ask questions again, but long ago they locked the door between them and their child by their irritability. Doors closed between child and parents are hard to reopen.

A child's curiosity involves all five senses. My daughter, Lois, was looking at a very fragile vase. I said to her, ''Look at it with your eyes only, it might break.'' Lois answered, ''But I can't see it unless I touch it with my fingers.'' This is so true for a child since he is learning through all his senses. Pity the poor child who gets into a place where he dare not touch anything. Pity the poor hostess too, whose little guest has not learned to touch things carefully, or to let things alone. Some years ago a survey of school children revealed that a large majority of children preferred the museums to the movies, especially the museums arranged for the children to do a lot of touching.

The whole of God's world of nature should be available to a child in reality or through books and museums. This is a world of wonder to a child. Two nine-year-old boys put a group of small ants into a glass box filled with sand. Then they put in a group of large ants and waited to see what would happen. They were entranced—and quiet for most of the day—as they watched a pitched battle, the ''clean up '' process, the reorganization of forces for work to be done. Later on when they came to the story of the behavior of ants in a school book they were excited indeed. They had already learned about it.

Curiosity is the beginning and the motivating power in all learning. For many children this capacity for curiosity is stifled by bungling adults who do not know how important a child's honest questions really are. Because a child's curiosity is so often blunted by his parents, school teachers have to take courses on motivation to know how to restore a child's desire for learning. Many a child is mentally absent, although physically present in school. The good teacher knows that the child's God-given curiosity has to be redeemed before he can learn properly.

This is what Jesus meant when He said, ''Blessed are those who hunger and thirst for righteousness, for they will be filled'' (Matt. 5:6). The child's curiosity about his world, about life, about God, when encouraged leads to this hunger and thirst for truth. Many adults are not filled because they have lost their capacity to hold anything. Jesus was talking about this same capacity in the parable of the sower (Matt. 13:1–8, 18–23). Jesus said the seeds sown on the hard footpath represented the message coming to a heart with no understanding whatever. ''The evil one comes and snatches away what was sown in the heart.'' Some ground was rocky. This represents the one who hears the message gladly, but it takes no root in him because he has no depth or capacity. In the thorny ground the good is choked out. The good ground represents the heart that is prepared or trained to respond to God.

A repetition of truths does not necessarily mean that the truths have been truly learned. Jesus said mere repetition and much saying of words do not count (Matt. 6:7). For too many years parents and teachers of religion were satisfied if the children could repeat verses from the Bible, or if they knew the catechism. But educators found what Jesus knew, that mere knowing of facts does not insure the living of the truths. In India we had an annual examination on the Sunday school lessons of the year. The examination was made out and sponsored by the National Sunday School Union. One girl in my Sunday school class decided to take the examination even though she had not been coming to church. She borrowed the quarterlies and studied very hard. Her paper was excellent—except it gave suspicious evidence of cheating. It could not be accepted. I asked her why she cheated. She said, "Because I wanted the Bible that was given to each one who passed!"

The desire for and the attitude toward the truth are of great importance. With the recognition of this insight, some educators went so far for a time as to say that only the attitude counted; that any accumulation of facts or Bible verses for young children was useless. They couldn't understand what they learned, so let them wait until they could understand what they were learning. "Memory work" was frowned upon, even through the age when children have a natural, though mechanical memory. So little boys knew the names of all the baseball players and all the cars on the road and little girls knew the names of all the movie stars, but intellectual eyebrows were lifted if the children knew the names of the books of the Bible!

In one home the family read the Twenty-third Psalm every day for a week. To their surprise their three-and-one-half-year-old by the end of the week knew the Psalm by heart. The mother was apologetic for fear someone would think she was so old-fashioned as to have her child commit Scripture to memory. I told her it was wonderful that her little girl knew the Psalm. The only objection I could see would be to force learning or in using Bible memorizing as means of punishment, as some foolish parents have done. Her little girl had learned the Psalm in line with all good teaching principles. Then she told me the rest of the story. Just before Christmas she and the little girl had gone shopping. Of course, a child wants everything she sees. The tune was "I want. I want." Mother kept saying they could not afford to buy everything they wanted. Finally after another "I want," the little girl stopped suddenly and exclaimed, "I want and want and want, but I mustn't want— because the Lord is my Shepherd." No one knows how much of God's truth a child can understand! Why deliberately keep it away from them? The Word of God should be a real part of a child's environment.

One Sunday I visited a nursery class. The teacher asked, "What verse did we learn last Sunday?" I thought she was foolish to expect little tots to remember so long, but a little blonde answered, "Let the little kiddies come unto Me." She not only remembered, but she understood. Who can object to her modern version?

When religious teachers got away from "content teaching" in the name of better methods, they aimed to keep the children "happy" in an atmosphere of love at home and at church. They thought character would develop naturally from a good environment. But a generation of such teaching revealed that no one drifts into character. When these children reached the age to think for themselves they didn't have any training to think religiously; neither did they have any training to be able to make choices. They had indeed drifted through a nebulous atmosphere. The drifting did not dispose of an inner conscience. And a conscience without content in moral thinking and without training in moral choosing is not a guide. It is an accuser that piles on to one's inner being undefined and sickening guilt. Some counselors tried unsuccessfully to deaden the conscience instead of giving it reasonable content to work by. The conscience must have a guide; it is only an inner voice. Those who know God's Word have the assurance that there are ultimate values and that these values are dependable. The conscience guided by the laws of God is a free conscience.

Today there is real concern among educational philosophers for ultimate values, for discernment concerning right and wrong, for the necessity that youth learn to distinguish for themselves in all moral values. "Good" and "bad" are no longer naughty words. Thinking educators are frightened at the results of a generation of "relative values" and of "attitudes" that change so easily when there is no content to give them meaning. Being momentarily happy may turn out to be an illusive experience with no enduring qualities, especially since happiness can never be an end in itself, but is only the result of an enduring relationship.

The secular philosopher says there are values to go by but he does not clearly define those values. Who will, unless those who know the Word of God do so? People turn to secondary or false values only because they do not know the real ultimates that have stood the test of the centuries. The people of God and of His Book never had a greater opportunity than they have today.

As I look back to my childhood, one of the greatest memories was of going to Grandfather's. He lived on a Pennsylvania farm that was written up in *Holiday* magazine some years ago. We do not wonder that the old stone house attracted modern writers; but Grandpa, as we called him, was not to be forgotten either. He was a good man and progressive for his day. Today he would be called ultraconservative and an authoritarian, but he was worthy of his authority. We grandchildren never resented him; we stood in awe of him; we behaved—period. He had a dry sense of humor too, even though he seemed so serious. I especially remember the day my brother William took the corncob out of a hole at the bottom of a sack of clover seed! William stood there entranced at the steady flow of the tiny, heavy seeds. Of course, Grandpa appeared out of nowhere. Without a word he picked William up and dunked him in a rain barrel around the corner and then went on his way. (William says he dunked him three times. The dear old man preached hard for *trine* immersion!) Anyway, that was Grandpa!

Breakfasts at Grandpa's are the occasions I remember best. The table was always loaded with ham, sausage, eggs, homemade bread, fruits, pies, etc. We children were always hungry but we had to sit patiently in front of all that food while Grandpa read a whole chapter from the Bible and prayed long enough for us to know that God was the head of that household. After all these years I would say that I learned from those breakfasts that the Bible is important and that worship of God is more important than eating of food.

By contrast, in later years, when church people went overboard to present to a child only what he could understand of the Bible and no more, they inadvertently taught that the Bible wasn't important because it wasn't used much.

The Bible is not only important, it is important for what it communicates of God's truth. The best of one's mind, as well as one's whole being, is necessary to understand its great truths. The printed page itself is not a charm. Children need to know that the Bible tells the story of real people who lived in a land far away; but they must not fall into the fantastic idea some children have, that Palestine is not on our earth. Four of our grandchildren had the privilege of living in the Holy Land for several years. The Bible stories are alive to them because Jerusalem and Bethlehem are just as real in their experience as New York and Washington.

By the time a child reaches the ''age of accountability'' he should know that the Bible is not a history book like his school history of the United States, but that it is the inspired story of the people chosen by God because they responded to Him more than any others. It is not a science book like the ones he studies in school because it is about *people*, and not mainly about *things*. It is about people and their relationships to God. However, the Bible, written so long ago, never does violence to any truth of the universe that man can discover, because it is about the God who created the universe. All truth is God's truth. The Bible tells about people who were part of the culture of their day, and yet above it, because of their faith in a living God.

Above all, the Bible tells about Jesus who came to live on this earth to show us what God is really like. Before He came it was hard for people to get the right idea about God. That is why Jesus had to come. Children must learn about the culture of the people in Jesus' time on earth, so that they can understand the meaning of His earthly relationships. They must know His daily life before they can get the force of God's love revealed in His death. It is harder to know the presence of the living Lord now if the earthly life of Jesus is not known. Without knowing Him, any religious commitment is merely a temporary emotional experience that will run a big chance of being laid aside with other childhood memories. There are already too many people who have stored away their Sunday school lessons with the toys of their childhood.

It is only as the mind is also trained to discern truth that anyone can continue through all of life with the Father God as revealed in Jesus Christ, the Author of all truth. *The trained mind is the tool with which God's grace can work efficiently for a fruitful life.*

I cannot close this chapter without sharing an article I have kept for thirty-five years, which, if followed, will lead a child toward discernment. It is by Constance Wardell and appeared in *Parent's Magazine* in October, 1928. She called it "A Young Mother Considers Religion":
"And so, my little son of the shining eyes, I would not paint you a picture of a white-bearded Santa Claus God, who waves a magic scepter from a golden throne above the skies. I shall tell you that the God of little children is much closer than that. He lives in your heart in a tiny flame that burns brightly and keeps you warm when you let it light the

way for you. When you are naughty it flickers low and makes you cold and unhappy. You must tend your lamp with the oil of loving kindness, true thoughts and friendly deeds.

"God did not wish you to live all by yourself in a solitary world. He made a multitude of other little children, black and white, red and yellow and brown, for you to live among and love and help. When you are unkind you are making their lamps burn low, too. He wants you to be His helper and work with Him to make a beautiful place for us all to live in.

"God gave you a little factory in your head so you can make thoughts all your own. He wants you to use it hard so that some day these thoughts will grow into big thoughts. No one else, not even Mother and Daddy, can think things out for you. But God and you in the little workshop of your brain, can make lovely dreams come true.

"God loves your strong little body, your husky arms and legs, your little mouth and eyes to life, too. He wants you to keep them clean and holy so that you may always be proud of the Temple in which He lives with you. If you are well and strong, your bright eyes will see many wonderful things, your mouth will say words that will help other people, your hands will do much work in a world where none can be lazy, your legs will run long races for high prizes.

"Just as you talk to Mother all day long and save some confidence for Daddy when he comes home at night, you will want to talk to God who is your Father. You will want to tell Him about your fun and your troubles, your happiness and your failures. He will whisper back to you in a quiet voice that you must be very quiet and still to hear. He will help you to keep the flame in your heart burning high and you will want to thank Him for His love and care, just as you hug Mother at the end of an especially happy day.

"So live and love, think and pray, my little son. Make better friends each new day with the other Father who is your High Companion. More careless for the things that money buys than for friendship with all mankind. And finally, recognize in those crystal clear thoughts of yours a lasting proof of your relationship to the Creator of all things."

Homework for Parents and Teachers—

- Make a study of your child's ability to think—or do you do all his thinking for him?
- What do you do with active children on a rainy Saturday?
- For one week, list all your child's questions. How did you answer them? Remember, you may not be able to answer every question but you must always answer the child.
- What is your child's attitude—and yours—toward new knowledge and new experiences?
- What place does the Bible have in your homelife?
- If older children express doubts, can you lead them into deeper faith without blunting their desire to think?

Chapter 11

Reverence for Worship

The Murray family had had an exciting day of sightseeing. They stopped for supper at a wayside table, but they were too close to the swiftly passing cars for tired children to settle down to proper eating. Mother Sally suggested moving to a quieter spot. So they packed up the food and drove on until they found a quiet place by a little stream away from the noisy highway. Again they set out their food. They all sighed with relief, and the boy who had been the most excitable before said with deep satisfaction, "This is just what I wanted." He didn't know he wanted quiet until he experienced it. Many a child never has enough quiet around him to be able to express his pleasure in it, yet this is one of the greatest needs of childhood. Without quiet experiences a child has a hard time ever learning to enter into an experience of worship.

Fénelon said, "How rare it is to find a soul quiet enough to hear God speak!" This is the reason most people do not hear the voice of God; they are never quiet long enough.

Too many homes are like TV programs; they have no silent periods whatsoever. If a child sits still for any length of time someone is sure to ask him, "What's the matter with you? Are you sick?" The chances are that the child who doesn't know how to be quiet at any time is the sick one, or is headed for sickness. One wise mother said, "What's the matter with loafing anyway?"

A family with five lively boys moved away from the distracting excitement of Pittsburgh to a gorgeous old house on top of a hill in the midst of space and woods far from the city. But even there in all that quietness the boys would get all "wound up." They had their own built-in excitement! One day when their father came home from work he saw that the boys were so "full of themselves" that they were getting too rough with one another. Remembering his Quaker background he called the boys into the big dining room around the fireplace and said, "Now we are going to sit here in silence for twenty minutes." This was new discipline for the boys and somehow they felt more sense of authority in the silence than in previous orders to be quiet. An order peremptorily given to "be still" will not *quiet* a child. Real quietness of spirit is achieved by cooperation only.

Remember, whatever a child learns he will incorporate into his play life, and what he plays he will learn. Playing a game of silence in preparation for the service at church is really wonderful training. "Who is big enough to keep quiet today?" or "How long can we play silence today?" are attractive invitations to a child for the "next game." Little four-year-old Kevin Miller was playing church. His father happened to hear the "call to worship." Kevin was standing in his little improvised pulpit and with lifted hand, he intoned,

> Holy is everywhere, Holy is here.
> Holy is everywhere, Holy is here.
> Holy is everywhere far and near.

In another home silence is practiced at the beginning of each meal, followed by a song of thanksgiving. When I was in this home the two-year-old broke the silence by saying joyously, "Sing Alleluia, Sing Alleluia." Somehow bickering is out of place at that family table. Family worship is continuous.

Sometimes it seems that the children are quicker to learn this requisite for worship than are adults. Our church life is often all activity. We rush into the words of prayer, we rush away. We shout at children to be quiet when we are never quiet ourselves. We do not know how to worship because we do not feel at home in the silence of God.

One of the values of silence is that we learn to listen. The mother listens even in her sleep for the sound of a new baby's cry so that she may meet his every need. Then when he can more or less take care of himself he can find no listening ear: everyone is too busy. But the need for the listening ear never ceases. A child comes home from school ready to tell of the day's happenings, but if his mother is not there ready to listen his confidence will pass. One young woman said to me, "The only listening ear I can find is the psychiatrist's and I have to pay him for it!"

But then, real listening is not cheap. Listening costs unhurried time: nearly all people are in a hurry. It requires a forgetfulness of self so that one can see into the heart of another. It requires love and understanding so that one can listen without condemnation. It requires patience to wait for the other one to find his own way as he bares his soul. It requires the presence of the Spirit of God so that healing faith may be given. In fact, God is the Great Listener. The person who can listen to the heart of another is the one who can open the door to God for the needy one.

Those who have experimented with children in listening to God have found that the children hear "God tell" them the thing they already know about right and wrong. This is no argument against such sharing in listening. Why shouldn't this be called the voice of God? How else can God reach through to a person than through the best that person knows? The difficulty is that the one who does not stop to think doesn't even know what his best thoughts are. Children today are bombarded with strong impressions (even the good ones) at such a rate of speed that they have no time to know themselves or anyone else. They need to know themselves to be ready to know God.

Young people at summer camps realize this need. One high-school girl asked, "How can we keep the spirit of our mountaintop experiences when we return to our hectic daily lives?" Invariably it is the vesper service in summer camp that means the most to boys and girls. Where prayer rooms are provided in summer conferences it is the high-school students who spend more time there than their elders. I have often seen the camp snack shop filled with middle-aged "fatties" after a night meeting while their teenage children were in the prayer room. One mother told me about visiting her nine-year-old boy at camp. They had had no religious experience together at home. The boy said to her, "Oh, Mother, the most wonderful thing has happened to me here. I've learned to pray. Come on, I want to show you our prayer room. It's in a cave on the mountainside." So he took her up the mountain path. When they reached the cave door, the "flag" was up and the boy explained, "We can't go in now, someone else is there. It's so quiet in there, I know now about God." From her child this mother learned more about God. At any age it seems that the young people can join with the little one who discovered, "This quiet is just what I wanted."

The love of beauty seems to be an integral part of the sense of worship. Children seem especially sensitive to the appeal of beauty. The lovely things of nature stir them easily to wonder. This inborn sense of wonder is quickly turned to reverence and worship. The little child who brings a crushed dandelion flower saying, "Pretty! Pretty!" is opening his heart to the beginnings of reverence and worship. We will hope that the adult to whom he offers the crushed flower will see the opening flower of worship in the child's heart rather than the "crushed weed." Some adults are stupidly blind, however, like the mother whose child came calling to her to look "at the pretty sky"; but she wanted to finish reading her book, so she scolded the child, "Let me alone so I can finish my story!" Simple joys shared in fellowship lead to reverence and worship.

The beauty of nature can bring great reverence to anyone who opens his eyes to see. Our daughter, Lois, had an unusual experience that meant much to her spiritually. She had come out from Washington, D.C. on the night bus to visit her aunt. The driver forgot to waken her as he passed my sister's house in the village. Five miles further she awoke and asked where they were. The bus driver apologized for not waking her, but put her off on a country road at three-thirty in the morning to walk back five miles all by herself! She wrote us, "I felt panicky and ready to cry until I decided the only thing to do was walk—the moon and God were good company. It's the first time, I think, that I actually held conversation with God. Anyway, it kept me from crying and helped me to cover five miles through woods and farms and barking dogs. And as I was walking, looking at the stars to keep my mind off the dogs, I saw the whole meteor phenomena! It started high in the heavens and looked just like an ordinary falling star until it started to burn. Then it got red, leaving a trail of silver and red sparks. Then the red turned green like burning copper and finally a brilliant blue silver like burning magnesium. Then it blew up in the sky, but I could see the red and blue tail falling toward the earth. It was one of the most beautiful and comforting sights I've ever seen. I wouldn't have missed it for anything!" I, her mother, still feel frightened at the thought of my young daughter on that lonely road at that hour of the night; but her astronomer daddy envies her view of the great phenomenon of that night.

When a child has a sense of worship he needs to share it and to be able to express it. If the family has the custom of singing together he will find real joy in singing "Alleluia," for children learn best by participation. If the parents express their own gratitude to God spontaneously throughout the day children will also learn to be thankful. Expressing gratitude in appreciation for one another is also an integral part of the spirit of thankfulness. Many people fail in their prayer life because they begin with petition, when true prayer really begins with praise *to* God. Many people bemoan the loss of the custom of *family worship* in the American home. They are thinking of a more or less formal experience in the home, like at my grandfather's breakfast table. But trying to imitate grandfather's methods will not insure a family worship experience. It may bring only guilt when it doesn't work well. Perhaps practicing "spiritual conversation" will open the door to the best way for the family to worship together today.

"Spiritual conversation" is what the Israelites practiced when they talked of God's goodness to them when they were sitting at home, while they walked on the road, when they lay down and when they got up. This is the way they led their children to the desire to worship.

The possibilities in spiritual conversation came to me several years ago when a friend invited about a dozen of us to her home for spiritual conversation. Usually we meet for prayer, we meet for Bible study and, in either case we feel guilty if we just talk about God and ourselves. This time we sat around a dining table with nothing on it but a beautiful centerpiece. It was so refreshing to talk about God and His goodness without feeling we ought to be doing something else. It turned out that we had more real prayer and more discernment of God's truth than often happens in the other kind of meeting.

I have seen this happen in other church groups who met for spiritual conversation. Perhaps this is what John Wesley's "class meetings" really were. The family is the natural unit for such an experience. I heard a minister in Chicago tell one time about his most precious childhood memory: every morning his father appeared before the family with the greeting, "This is the day the LORD has made; let us rejoice and be glad in it" (Ps. 118:24). These words set the mood of joy for the morning meal and for the day.

When the family can converse about the things of God, family worship becomes a natural result and not an artificial form imposed on unwilling participants. In such a family, symbols and rituals take on real meaning. One need not be afraid about the children not understanding the symbols and rituals. The real family experience together in worshipful living interprets the symbols and rituals to children. Some say that rituals and symbols get through to the unconscious with deep meanings that are lasting and beyond expression. At least they cling to the memory and are there for new meanings to develop.

Many families hold hands around the table for the time of the grace. This is a lovely symbol of family unity before the Lord. Besides, it helps the little ones feel that they are participants, as well as making it easier for them to be quiet. One young couple put their little baby on the bed with their arms around her as they knelt each night for their evening prayer. Even though their eyes were closed the little one was within the circle of their arms and a part of their worship. No one knows how much gets across to a small child. They usually seem to understand more than we think they do! We must not run the risk of empty religious space in their lives. They learn soon about the American flag and TV commercials, why deprive them of the symbols that can lead them to ask the questions we want them to ask and which can lead them to God?

For a small child prayer is a ritual, but it is a loved experience. Little prayers learned by heart and spontaneous prayers are a joy to every child. He will get the real meaning of the importance from the lives of his parents. Rituals connected with birthdays, a special family night, Christmas, Easter, etc., become very dear to a child and remain with him always.

Above all, we need to remember that worship is more than a form, more than an attitude, more than an "atmosphere," it is an encounter with and an experience *toward God*. It is an experience of a growing relationship. Little Mary Jane had the right idea when she asked, "Is this church, telling God how glad we are just because He is?" Worship is worshiping Someone.

It seems children understand more about this unseen One than we dream they do. A little boy had been told by his mother that God was with him always. One night he told her, "God even goes to school with me. He sits with me at my desk and, you know, Mother, it isn't even crowded!'' The home experience carried over for him into his school life.

It is not only the special ''religious'' moments in the family life that have spiritual significance, but *all good family experience is religious experience.* The religious values are communicated there: love, beauty, reverence, justice, courage, faith, joy, kindness, helpfulness, sharing, cooperation, obedience. All these are involved in the training of reverence for worship. But possibly the most neglected necessary quality is the respect for one another and even for another's things. It is too easy in our busy lives to forget that a child has feelings, *and* his possessions are important. He has a hard time knowing how important he is to God if his parents do not have this same respect for him. He must learn also how important parents are or he will have a hard time knowing about the authority of truth and the authority of God.

Any child will learn to worship God who lives his daily life with adults who worship Him.

Homework for Parents and Teachers—

■ Take inventory of the spiritual status of your family life.
■ Start where you are for improvement and do not be discouraged. Talk about it with the family.
■ Perhaps a ''wonder table'' would help: a place for the children to place the things they find that excite their wonder.
■ Lead from the wonder of the child to the God who created these wonders. After you start toward God He will draw you on.

Chapter 12

The Goal of the Preparation:
Christian Character

There is never any argument against *lived out* religion. Children who resent the religion of their childhood do it because they have a memory only of a *profession* of religion that was not a part of daily life. It is the profession without the living that creates the hard, empty arrogance that passes sometimes for orthodoxy, and which turns children against the God who has been so grossly misrepresented.

Matthew, once a student of mine, was one of eight children. In his home Christian character was taken seriously; it was to be lived. As a young man Matthew wrote: "My parents endured much hardship and we children learned to get along without an abundance of money or possessions. It is fascinating for a child to awaken gradually to understand the situations and surroundings into which he is born. I can remember that I quickly came to understand that since I was a preacher's son, I was automatically expected to be different from other children of the community. Our parents taught us that true Christians are not of this world. We were told to avoid worldly things and to seek always for the good and the true. Some ministers' children complain about being told to be different from other children, but I have no regrets in that area. Perhaps this was because, although I thought of my father as authority, I always remember him as being very humble. So I believe this teaching about being 'different' was a wholesome kind of teaching which kept my actions more respectable and my conscience a little stronger. Probably the most influential factor which contributed to my spiritual life was my early home life. The teachings and spiritual habits and attitudes of my parents, the constant application of Christian principles to all areas and situations in life made Christianity an everyday thing to me. Honesty, fairness, forgiveness, tolerance, Christian love and devotion were stressed at all times in word and action."

I once heard several ministers discussing some bad feelings that had arisen between some ministers in the area. Then one minister added, "But you know we are all human." I did not know why this statement made me feel sad until I realized that he was *defending* human weakness. There is only one thing to do with our failures when we see them, and that is to *confess* them. Matthew's father was a successful father because he was never defensive of weakness but he was humble, and he took seriously every requirement for Christian character.

The apostle Paul said the Christian is a *new creature,* which means that he is a *new person,* belonging to a new family. The "inherited characteristics" of the new family, the family of God, outweigh the disposition inherited from the earthly family. Most people who are not new creatures after they join the church fail to change because they take their first inheritance more seriously than their second, or new inheritance in Christ. They therefore excuse their lack of growth by blaming their parents instead of confessing their earthly weaknesses and accepting the grace of God available to make them real members of the new family.

Some people hide behind a faulty theological interpretation of what God wants to do for His children. They talk about "imputed grace" as if it were a garment to put on a dirty body to cover the dirt rather than the miracle of grace it is which *intrinsically* changes the person so that he can truly become "more and more like Jesus." If we do not have this much faith in the grace of God, then the grace cannot do its full work in our lives.

A little child is at the beginning of finding out what he can do "all by his lone." He learns to feed himself, to dress himself, to go to the store for mother, to study his own lessons at school, to drive a car, and then to make his own living. If he compares himself only with others he may think he is as good as anyone else. And he probably is as good as "the next one." But if he reads the Gospels and sees the picture that Jesus gave of Christian character and if he takes seriously what Jesus says, he will know that this kind of character he cannot create all by his "lone." Then he will truly know what the limits of human achievement are and wherein man needs the power and grace of God.

In religious education circles the debate has swung back and forth through the years on whether Christian character is achieved by human effort or merely accepted by divine grace. Some thought character development depended entirely on education, while others went to the other extreme to say it depended only on God. The latter forgot that God created man with the power of choice and the need to assume the responsibility of his choices. He who waits for God to do it all is lazy and arrogant; he is one who is *professing* without *being*. But he who learns cooperation with God will find the joy of God's gift of power for living.

We, as parents and teachers, must know the Christian goal in character so that we will recognize our own needs; then we will be able to guide our children. Jesus came to reveal this to us.

The basic quality of God is *love:* "Dear friends, let us love one another, for love comes from God. Everyone who loves has been born of God and knows God . . . because God is love . . . We love because he first loved us" (1 John 4:7,8,19). Since Jesus came to reveal God, He revealed the real meaning of love in His own life on earth. He expected us to have this same love: "A new command I give you: Love one another. As I have loved you, so you must love one another. All men will know that you are my disciples if you love one another" (John 13:34,35).

Paul said that no religious experience is of any value whatsoever if it does not spring from love and is not permeated with love. His definition of orthodoxy begins and ends with love. He describes this love in everyday terms (1 Cor. 13). Because it is never filled with self-pity it *endures* long. It is always *kind.* It is *never jealous.* (Webster says this means it is "never pained by preference given to another.") Love is *not out for personal display,* it is *not conceited* or *unmannerly; it is not self-seeking,* therefore it is *not irritable.* Love *never nurses hurt feelings.* Love sides happily with the *truth* always.

Only when we see this love as realistic and functional for everyday relationships can we understand the seeming paradox of the Beatitudes that Jesus gave as the picture of Christian character. In them we find our goal for Christian character. The Beatitudes describe the attitudes of the growing Christian. The attitudes mentioned are not the ones we usually think of as bringing happiness, but in each case the person is called *blessed.* If we accept the way of Jesus as being practical, the combinations in the Beatitudes will not seem incongruous at all, but altogether logical. It all depends on how much we believe in Jesus. Needless to say, this is not man's natural way of thinking. It is God's thinking. The first Beatitude about the *poor in spirit* seems like a strange beginning. This quality of character is the last thing learned by most Christians. To Jesus it was of prime importance for it is the *key to the entrance into the kingdom:* "for theirs is the kingdom of heaven." "These are they who sense spiritual poverty" (Modern Language). They know that in themselves they are poor; they have no reason to be arrogant or proud; they feel no need to demand their rights or to seek prestige or honor. They discern the real values of life. Being poor in spirit includes the motivating curiosity of a child, his creative imagination, and his inspired push toward growth. Absence of haughty self-sufficiency and conceit does not leave a person destitute of dignity, but gives him the courage of a man secure in his relationships. No wonder he is blessed. This humility is inner strength, a real dignity that never needs to pretend or to flaunt itself.

"Blessed are *those who mourn,* for they will be comforted." This is the quality of sensitiveness to others. Love is always vulnerable. When suffering and loss come there is no room for self-pity, no asking the disastrous question: "Why should this happen to me?" There is no succumbing to sorrow or failure, no effort at escape from pain, but a courageous faith in the God of love. The result: the pain is lessened or leaves entirely and comfort comes to bless the mourner. This attitude will eliminate all tantrums and all despair.

"Blessed are the *meek* (or gentle), for they will inherit the earth." This is the quality of being poor in spirit as it manifests itself to other people. It is easier to be humble toward God than it is toward people, especially arrogant ones, but the test of the first is in the latter. Meekness is never tame resignation to others; which would be a self-centered attitude. It is rather an *understanding thoughtfulness* of others. This quality of life sets one free from the competitive rat race that drives so many people to distraction these days. It opens the hearts of even the hardhearted for it takes away their fear of being walked over. If the earth is the Lord's, why shouldn't those who have His Spirit inherit it? The meek are strong—in the Lord. No wonder they are blessed. Anyway, who owns the earth—those with real-estate deeds in safety deposit boxes or those who enjoy the beauty of God's earth?

Being poor in spirit, able to endure suffering, meek and gentle toward others does not mean at all that one is passive or complacent. Deep in their hearts the nonbelievers know this, for they are often afraid of those whom they cannot touch with their threats of manipulative power. This inner strength is a positive strength, it is an outreaching attitude and not one of withdrawal. The positive desire of this strength is shown in "Blessed are those who *hunger and thirst after* righteousness, for they will be filled." This is love of truth and the ability to discern right from wrong. It is an attitude readily fostered in a growing child, for he is already full of curiosity.

This love of truth needs an accompanying discernment because it is easy to overconcentrate on a chosen goal. Jesus said, "Seek first his kingdom and his righteousness, and all these things (physical needs) will be given to you" (Matt. 6:33). By discriminating between first things and secondary things one can avoid the stress of becoming ruthless, censorious, and condemnatory. To offset this tendency Jesus said that an integral part of the earnest Christian's attitude is that of *mercy*. The merciful show the love of God in their attitude toward others, and so make tender the hearts of others. In this they find mercy is reciprocated and they receive a great blessing. The devout Christian's problem is how to have strong convictions and still be merciful. The parent and teacher find it difficult to be stern concerning the truth and still tender toward the child who errs. This combination of strength and mercy is possible through His Spirit.

"Blessed are the *pure in heart,* for they will see God." The pure in heart are the sincere and single-minded in their service to God. One cannot be a "good self" on Sunday and a "worldly self" during the week. Only those who follow Christ with a *whole heart* can know God. This beatitude combines all the previous ones, making life whole. Some Christians feel so far from God because they are still double-minded; only the pure in heart are blessed by knowing Him.

In the next beatitude we go from the experience of knowing God to being a partner in His concern for others: "Blessed are the *peace-*

makers, for they will be called sons of God.'' Paul said it beautifully: ''God was reconciling the world to himself in Christ, not counting men's sins against them. And he has commited to us the message of reconciliation'' (2 Cor. 5:19). God's sons do not condemn others but they seek to bring them together in Christ.

Peacemakers often run into trouble with the people who seek prestige and power, who manipulate strife in order to gain power. When this peacemaker seeks nothing for himself, he will not mind the trouble that comes because his whole interest is in the work of God, and so he will be blessed. This has no reference to those who are persecuted for their own shortcomings. Martyrs never know they are martyrs! The result of this beatitude is the same as that of the first one: ''for theirs is the kingdom of heaven.''

So we have seen the picture of Christian character as delineated by Jesus Christ Himself. It is one of inner peace and wholeness, of unbroken relationship with God, of the outreach of love to friend and foe. Jesus said it is as if the Christian were *salt.* Salt is stimulating, cleansing, flavorful, and it protects against decay. He also said it is as if he were *light.* Light makes it possible for others to be able to see what is right. The light is not ours. The flame is not ours. It is His. Its witness is of Him.

The Christian courage to be ''light'' and ''salt'' in the world, irrespective of personal consequences, has great appeal to juniors and young people. Even the little ones are attracted to the spirit of courage. This courage to be God's child in a discordant world is of the quality of the cross. The cross has for too long been only a ritualistic symbol in Christianity. Jesus meant it for everyday. ''He who saves his life shall lose it, but he who loses his life for my sake shall find it.'' The clue to the secret of Christian character is in this amazing statement of Jesus. We will find out in the next chapter what it means; and if we do not find out, our children will never find their way to life and we can lose ours.

Homework for Parents and Teachers—

- Have each member of the family make a list of the characteristics of Christian character.

- Have each member make a list of his own shortcomings and what is being done about them.
- Share these with one another.
- Read aloud together daily for a week the 8th chapter and the 12th chapter of Romans.

Chapter 13

The Secret of Character Development

A bewildered religious educational leader of the Jews, who was attracted to Jesus, came to Him one night to find out the secret of His ministry. Nicodemus did see Him as a man come from God. The signs were there, but Jesus did not have the right degrees and the right training. Yet, on the other hand, He was getting results with the people. So this graduate from the best religious education school of the day was perplexed; he thought he knew the answers, but here was something beyond him.

The answer Jesus gave him was not on *what* to teach or *how* to teach it, but something much deeper than either of these: how to become a member of the family of God. This is something "from above" and is beyond what man can do for himself. This "seminary graduate" of the day was still mystified for he was still thinking in earthly terms; while Jesus was talking of a new birth through the Spirit that changed one's relationship entirely, making him a member of a spiritual kingdom.

Another day Jesus was talking to the people and some religious snobs were listening in on what was going on (". . . those confident of their own righteousness and *looked down on everybody*"). Jesus told them a parable of one of the men from the religious education school who went up to the temple to pray. He was a "good man," respectable and honorable, and a prominent man in the community, but he knew it! When he compared himself with one who collaborated with the occupying army in Israel, he could not help but know that he was "a better man." Yet Jesus said the collaborator went home "made righteous." The outer difference in these two men was all to the advantage of the prominent churchman, but the inner attitude made the real difference to God. While the "good man" told God how good he was, the "sinner" knew his guilt, contrasted himself with God and asked for forgiveness (see Luke 18:9–14).

Both the church leader and the despised man went up to the temple to worship. I wonder what the prominent man would have said if he had found out that the despised one found more favor with God than he did. Still his desire was to be a "good" man and to be of service to mankind! The flaw in his character had developed so subtly that he was entirely unaware of it. He was a proud, self-centered man, the star of his own drama—and pleased with himself! More than that, he was spiritually blind and he did not know it. Dr. Fritz Kunkel called such egocentricity "condensed darkness."

We all want to be *real* persons. We want the "life abundant" that Jesus promised, but the usual human dilemma is that in seeking for fulfillment we become the center of our own world, the end of our own existence and we find nothing at the end but blasted hopes and despair. God knew how easy it is for man to miss the way, so He, the Creator, sent His Son to tell us the real secret for fulfillment of life. Jesus Himself lived it so He knew by experience that it was the right way. He said, "Whoever wants to save his life will lose it" (Matt. 16:25). Even for Himself He said, "If I testify about Myself, My testimony is not valid, there is another who testifies in my favor, and I know that His testimony about me is valid" (John 5:31). Paul wrote to the Romans that "Christ did not please himself" (Rom. 15:3).

With all that Jesus said and showed in His life about fulfillment of self many still lose the way. A handsome young minister preached much on the fulfillment of life, then he heard that every person has "undiscovered areas of his inner self." He went to a man who promised to help him unearth his inner treasures of self (at a price!). What an exciting time he had! He said it was a thrilling adventure to discover all the things he did not know about his inner life. In fact, he became intoxicated with himself. His sermons became *self* revelations. His family and his church became merely an audience for the stage performance in which he starred. He did the things a father should do for his children but he did not see the children; he was watching his "father heart"! His congregation got tired of hearing about their minister's inner self. They wanted to hear about God, so they asked him to leave.

We will save a lot of time lost in searching if we start out with believing what Jesus said, "If anyone would come after me, *he must deny himself* and take his cross daily and *follow me*. For whoever wants to save his life will lose it, but *whoever loses his life for me,* will save it" (Luke 9:23,24). In the human way of thinking this denial of self is an enigma and a paradox, even a contradiction.

Religious people of all ages and of every faith have recognized what a burden *self* can be in their efforts to find God. Many have tried every way they could think of to get rid of self, even to the most gruesome ascetic practices. Some, in despair, have concluded that only by suicide could they make it. The despair comes because they try to get rid of self by their own efforts in human strength only.

It is not surprising that those who never heard of the prior initiative of God to help man will think that their spiritual progress depends on their own efforts. Such was the case with a young prince in India about five hundred years before Christ. (This was about the time of the restoration of Judah after the Babylonian captivity.) Young Prince Siddhartha, better known as Buddha, became greatly distressed about the suffering and futility of life. He studied Hindu wisdom but it did not satisfy him. He tried a strict life of physical hardship but this was futile. After six years of deep searching, "enlightenment" came to him. He found satisfaction in his clarification of thought. He saw that there are three paths which a man may choose: (1) seek worldly pleasure; (2) the path of mortification; (3) the middle path. He chose the middle path and said it alone would lead to selflessness and peace.

According to Buddha, on this middle path there are "four noble truths": (1) to live means to suffer. Some suffering cannot be avoided; (2) *suffering is caused by man's desires,* many of them selfish and grasping; (3) to do away with suffering one must give up self-centered craving; (4) discipline to *get rid of desire* in order to get rid of evil.

This was great discernment for one who did not have any revelation of a God who reaches out to man. Through the centuries followers of Buddha have disciplined themselves to get rid of desire, *all* desire, good as well as bad. Many have sought and waited most earnestly for a religious experience they call "enlightenment." Buddhists who give themselves to this mystical search are called *Zen* Buddhists. It is challenging to read about these people in their religious earnestness before Christ came, and even in the Far East today where they have not had enough witness about Christ to know what more He has to give.

The popularity of this Zen Buddhism in American religious life today is a strange phenomenon. Many Christian church people who are dissatisfied with their undisciplined spiritual lives are seeking deeper experience of God through the disciplines of Zen Buddhism. This means they do not know of the true mystical experience of the indwelling Christ through the Holy Spirit, and of the glorious disciplines of love and grace because He is our strength and life. The son of Mahatma Gandhi in Africa is a devout Buddhist. He challenged a Y.M.C.A. secretary by saying that the religion that made the best men would win out in the world. They had been discussing the merits of Buddhism and Christianity. One thing is certain: a lazy, half-consecrated Christian has no witness to a disciplined person of any other faith. No words are ever enough. People want something that makes a difference in life and character.

The renunciation of self is the *end purpose* of life for the Zen Buddhist, but for the Christian it is the *beginning* that opens his life to God. The Christian does not get rid of self to be worthy of God. Jesus said, "Follow Me," so the Christian follows Christ and lets self go. The denial of self one hundred per cent is just as necessary for a Christian but it is only half of his experience. The other side of his action is *following Christ* and the self-renunciation is incidental to this following and for the purpose of this following. When one renounces self in order to follow Christ he will not get caught in the meshes of the darkness of egocentricity.

For the Christian there is a real self that does not need to be denied. This self finds fulfillment in the life abundant when the *false* self is denied. In the letter to the Galatians Paul describes the desires the Christian must get rid of. All of these desires belong to the false self: adultery, unchastity, impurity, lewdness, idolatry, magic, animosities, hatred, jealousy, bad temper, dissensions, a factional spirit, heresies, envy, drunkenness, carousings. When God comes into a life the false self is displaced, killed, but this is not the end. *All the good desires are now released unhampered for fulfillment.* The new list of emotions and desires are the *fruit of the Spirit:* love, joy, peace, an even temper, kindness, goodness, fidelity, gentleness, self-control. The new disposition is *given* to the one who becomes a son of God. It is inheriting the characteristics of the new family. This is life abundant.

It *takes time for the real self to grow* even after the false self is denied, but there is an abundance of life-growing power available to everyone who follows Christ. God gives us time "until we all reach unity in the faith and in the knowledge of the Son of God and become mature, attaining to the whole measure of the fullness of Christ" (Eph. 4:11–16). "For this very reason, make every effort to add to your faith goodness; and to goodness, knowledge; and to knowledge, self-control; and to self-control, perseverance; and to perseverance, godliness; and to godliness, brotherly kindness; and to brotherly kindness, love. For if you possess these qualities in increasing measure, they will keep you from being ineffective and unproductive in your knowledge of our Lord Jesus Christ. But if anyone does not have them, he is nearsighted and blind, and has forgotten that he has been cleansed from past sins. Therefore, my brothers, be all the more eager to make your calling and election sure. For if you do these things, you will never fall (2 Peter 1:5–11).

Not only does it take time to grow into completeness of Christian character, but it takes *continuous applied choosing* on the part of the one who has given up the old false self for the new real self. With God's grace through the Holy Spirit this is possible. "Since, then, you have been raised with Christ, set your hearts on things above. . . . Set your minds on things above, not on earthly things. Put to death, therefore, whatever belongs to your earthly nature: sexual immorality, impurity, lust, evil desires, and greed, which is idolatry. . . . But now you must rid yourselves of all such things as these: anger, rage, malice, slander, and filthy language from your lips . . . . since you have taken off your old self with its practices and have put on the new self, . . . Let the peace of Christ dwell in you richly" (Col. 1:1–10, 16).

We have seen (in chapter 6) that *giving love* is the practical way of life; it is the way to understand God and it is the only way to be His child. Now we see also that the way of giving love is the only way for the true development of one's own real self. No one ever loses what is best for himself when he does for another what is best for the other person. This is hard to see in the midst of a difficult situation, but any other way of life leads to the fostering of a false self. The false self always chokes out the real self.

With this picture of the self as it develops into Christian maturity we have the goal in mind toward which everything in the growing child should be directed. In every relationship with the child, the parent and the teacher have one basic question to keep in mind: "In this situation what shall I do to help this child to be his best self, remembering always that I want him to be God's child?" Every step in training, in all daily relationships is a step toward this goal *or* in opposition to it.

Among devout oriental peoples the question is not asked, "How much can a child understand?" Rather, he is taught in *every phase* of his life. There are morning and evening rites, there are eating rites, and even the washing of hands has a religious significance. The child is not requested or ordered to follow these rites; the whole family takes it for granted that these things will be done. The children learn from the whole family about what is considered important. Their religious beliefs and customs are not tacked on to life, they *are* life. Self-renunciation is so important to a Buddhist that in some countries a four-year-old boy is taken through a special self-renunciation ceremony. The little fellow is dressed up in fine new clothes that would delight the heart of any child. But his joy is short-lived, for then the beautiful clothes are taken away from him, his head is shaved and he is taught about the worthlessness of all such finery (whether he can understand the words or not). After this the boy is robed in plain monk's robes and taken out begging with a beggar's bowl. This is only a first step toward a life of learning about renunciation.

The people of other faiths know what they want their children to learn. We Christian parents must face the question: *do we know what we want our children to learn?*

Most parents get so much satisfaction out of parenthood in the years when their children are entirely *dependent* upon them, they are often blind to the fact that the goal of life is that each child grow into *independence.* As he matures, his parents cannot go to school for him, they cannot get married for him, they cannot do his life work for him, they cannot have an experience of God for him. They can only *get him ready* for these responsibilities of life which he must go through himself.

True independence comes most easily to the child who has known the security of complete dependence upon a consistent love when he needed it. This kind of family love has accepted him for himself and has helped him find himself within the security of this love relationship. It is difficult for him to find himself unless his environment sets him free for the search. The search is a way of disciplined direction under the guidance of his parents. His growth will be evident in the ways he learns to help himself and to do things for himself. No wise adult will do for a child what he can do for himself. (If he does, the child will soon give up and let him do it!)

A child's great asset to growth is his natural inner propulsion toward learning new skills and discovering new things in his environment. He is ever pushing out the limits of his environment, but it is his parents who must have the wisdom to know where those limits should be. He learns to stand on his own feet, to crawl, to walk. He wants to touch and see everything for himself, but in each new area he has not yet learned where dangers lie. His parent-set boundaries need to be out far enough for him to have freedom for experimentation but not too far out beyond his responsible learning. He must learn to feed himself, no matter what a mess he makes at first. He must learn to dress himself, and mother must reckon with the time it takes him to do it. I was visiting in a home one day where the little boy had just learned that morning to tie the lace in his shoe. In the half hour I was there he untied and retied his shoe five times. His mother did not know what an important day this was in her little boy's life, so the repeated act made her "nervous," she said!

The child will learn to talk, he will learn to say no as well as yes. As he comes to a new consciousness of himself as a separate individual, he will enter a seeming self-centeredness. But it is really a healthy self-centeredness that is only a station on the road to self-autonomy and to self-realization. (The only trouble is that too many people never learn to go beyond this self-centeredness which is a sign of growth at three but a sign of death at forty!) Parents who are wise in helping a child experiment with his no's will help him by fostering every good interest he has in things outside himself. He needs to find his own initial identity and autonomy without thinking of himself as a star. Unconditional love that never casts him out even when he needs correction, will carry him through to the day when he can lose himself not only in "things" but in "others" without feeling that he has to defend himself against them.

A child's no is evidence of his dawning autonomy of self which he is unconsciously impelled to protect if it is challenged. Too much freedom or too much coercion will disturb the development of his dawning selfhood. The developing self has to be able to say no before a genuine yes can be said. And so one day he finds out that he is somebody in himself who can speak for himself. He no longer says, "Johnny is hungry" but "I am hungry!"

Anything that fastens a child's attention on himself, so that he wants to be the *center of attention* is no help to proper self development. There is nothing in which otherwise good parents fail more regularly than in *talking about their children in their presence!* His antics, smart sayings, and misbehaviors are exploited before the family and even before strangers. A bride and groom were visiting in a home when the three-year-old came in with his pottie and sat on it in front of the guests. His mother and the guests laughed—out of embarrassment, but that evening the mother delightedly told the story to her husband—in front of the child. Of course, the little fellow did the same stunt when the next guests came. It was hard for the child to understand why he was spanked this time. Why should it be entertaining the first time and naughty the second time?

Another mother did not know what was happening to her little girl with beautiful red curls until the day a guest came who made no remark about the curls. Then the little girl whispered to her mother, "The lady didn't see my curls yet, shall I mention them to her?" The mother saw that the child was getting too self-centered because of her hair, and since she could not control the remarks of strangers, she cut off the curls!

While a child is learning to know himself as an individual he must also learn to know others as individuals. He is important to his parents, but so are the other children. As he learns to think of others' needs he will not mind so much the limits he must face for himself.

By the time a child has his relationships balanced between himself as a separate individual and his family, it is time for him to go to school and then he has to learn this lesson all over again in relation to all the other children who also face the same problem, and to the new adults who are placed in authority over him. He has a real struggle to find his real world. He may tell tall tales as he seesaws between fantasy and reality. He will develop a deaf ear to parents who talk too much. He may even run away from home as did eight-year-old Owen. When his mother went to awaken him in the morning she found a note on the pillow instead of a sleeping boy. After several anxious hours the telephone rang and a familiar voice said, "I am out at Grandfather's farm; if you want to find me you can come to get me!" The next time he threatened to run away his mother said "I'll help you pack your bag." He decided to stay at home! One understanding person can melt away the rebellion that complicates the search for one's identity.

While a child is trying to find his own strength in relation to others he will often try to establish himself by fighting. Sometimes it will be only good-natured exuberant tussling. A mother who interferes in a tussling game will find herself rebuked for spoiling the fun, but if the boys are really fighting they will look guilty. Usually, dependable boys can work out the issue between them without interference, even if they are fighting. But it is an entirely different matter when a father tries to make his son fight. I was in a home where the father tried to do this. The boy was so interested in people and things that he did not need to fight in order to hold his own. He had the respect of his little friends and he had a sense of dignity that others did not seem to want to attack. The only thing that bewildered him was his father's attempt to shame him for not fighting.

Fathers think little boys must fight to be manly; mothers don't want them to fight, and try to keep them from it. The issue comes up in every gathering of parents. Christian parents should seek for a Christian answer. Do we want our son to be in constant competitive conflict and ill will with others or do we want him to learn to understand and work with others? Does he have to win *over* someone to find his own security? If so, is it real security? We want our children to learn that there is more heroism in moral courage than in brute force. Then every pertinent incident will be part of that lesson.

A sense of ownership is also an accompaniment of growing selfhood. This ownership must be honored, for honesty and respect for the property of others are not possible without it. This includes piggy banks! A mother in Chicago called me to come to her home. She was in despair because her son had stolen a sum of money from the office where he did odd jobs after school. He had never done anything like this before. It turned out that he was greatly frustrated because his mother had "taken" his savings which he had hidden in a bureau drawer. She had not consulted with the boy before she paid the household bills with his money! He was going to buy a bicycle and she had taken his money! How can a child have respect for himself or his possessions if his parents don't respect him? To this boy what his mother did was stealing just as much as when he took money from the office. And his stealing was rebellion against his mother's injustice.

There is no question about the needs of a child for love and affection, for belonging, for acceptance, for understanding, for a sense of achievement, but the test of whether these emotional needs have been met in a Christian way comes when the child becomes an integral member of a group outside the home. If his needs have been met in the home as they should have been, the child will never have to lean on the group for security, nor will he have to yield to the group against his own inner convictions in order to have acceptance. He will be able to be an autonomous individual within the group, or in spite of the group and its possible pressures upon him.

Every person needs both *togetherness* and *separateness* in order to develop his best selfhood. When togetherness is achieved at the expense of separateness a person feels smothered, as if he could not do his own breathing. The child who was smothered at home will let himself be smothered in the group away from home, and he will think he is independent when he is only rebelling against his home. If a child gains separateness at the expense of togetherness he will only be isolated from others. In either case his real self has not become autonomous or whole.

A balance must be maintained between the two so that a child does not feel it necessary to flee from the crowd *or* to fear aloneness.

This balance can be maintained only as there is commitment to God. This commitment should be made at least by the early teen years. Paul expresses the balance in these needs in relation to the commitment to God: "With eyes wide open to the mercies of God, I beg you, my brothers, as an act of intelligent worship, to give Him your bodies, as a living sacrifice, consecrated to Him and acceptable by Him. *Don't let the world around you squeeze you into its mould, but let God remould your minds from within,* so that you may prove in practice that the plan of God for you is good, meets all His demands and moves toward the goal of true *maturity*" (Rom. 12:1, 2 Phillips).

We have heard so often that the individual person cannot develop alone, that personality develops only in relationship. The argument for this statement has usually been that the individual needs the group's acceptance or he will have no sense of worth. One church leader, some years ago, even went so far as to say that it is better to do what the crowd does in order to be one of them, than it is to stand alone with a clear conscience, if the latter means being a "square." As a result of this emphasis many young people are stranded when alone. They cannot stand up alone. It was this kind of youth who could be brainwashed during the war. When the group changed they changed with it.

There is a real need for the group, but it is not for acceptance or support. It is for learning to *love.* If the secret of love is in giving, if the secret of personality fulfillment is in giving, how can one give unless he has someone to whom to give? The Christian's security is in his relationship to God, his fulfillment is in his outgoing service to others, not as a benefactor but because love, through God's grace, has become intrinsic in his life. When the Christian has to stand alone he is more conscious of the group's need than of his difference from them. He will not feel threatened by their opposition or criticism, or be defensive of his own position. God's acceptance gives the needed security and dignity, and his concern for the ones he loves gives him the winning humility he needs to be able to stand alone and still be one among them. When one has this relationship with others he will wake up to the fact that he is a real person with a self all his own—his own *and* God's own. In this he will find life abundant.

If parents and teachers do not know the secrets of God's laws for character development, how can they lead the children in the way of truth?

Homework for Parents and Teachers—

- How many of your actions and reactions are out of self-reference?
- Make a note of every time you talk about a child in his presence. Note what happens to him.
- Study your own inner feeling after you have defended yourself at another's expense and contrast it with the times you admitted your wrong as you were concerned in love for the other one.
- Guard the integrity of every child in your care.

Part III

The Gift of Life

*I have come that they may have life, and have
it to the full.*
John 10:10

*Unless a man is born again, he cannot see
the kingdom of God.*
John 3:3

*Don't you know that you yourselves are
God's temple and that God's Spirit lives in
you?*
1 Corinthians 3:16

*. . . strengthen you with power through his
Spirit in your inner being, so that Christ may
dwell in your hearts through faith.*
Ephesians 3:16,17

*So then, just as you did receive Christ Jesus
as Lord, continue to live in him.*
Colossians 2:6

Chapter 14

The Rebirth

When a child has been reared in a Christian home and in a Christian church, when the temple of his mind and heart has with deep reverence been prepared for holy occupancy; the time has come when he will inevitably have his own personal encounter with the Lord of Life. This encounter will not be with a stranger, for he has already learned to love Him. It will not be an encounter like a prodigal adult would have that would involve a complete change of direction and pattern of life; but it will involve just as definite a decision and just as definite a commitment to the Savior. For when the time comes that a child or youth knows there are two ways of life and he is responsible enough to choose the right way to life—or the wrong way to death, he is old enough to make his decision for Christ.

Many young people do not come to this decision when they should because parents and teachers often do not realize how important these early decisions are and how serious a matter it is to be ten or thirteen years old.

It is interesting and strange that all primitive peoples have counted the early adolescent years to be extremely important. Every early primitive culture initiated the youth into adult responsibilities and privileges. The goal of maturity was all important to them. These rites emphasized a break with childhood that centered in the close relationship with the mother. They tested the physical and moral strength of the youth, and usually contrived by ascetic practices, certain "spiritual emotional experiences" that would impress the young people. Most important of all was the instruction entrusted to each coming generation to carry on their heritage. Among the Hindus this initiation is even called "second birth" and so the initiate is called a "twice born."

Among many peoples, girls also undergo an initiation ceremony. I once had the privilege of attending the *navjote* ceremony of the Parsi girl who lived next door to us. (The Parsi religion began 1000 years before Christ.) This ceremony takes place at about seven years of age.

The priest begins the ritual by lighting a fire and chanting the watch-word of their faith: "I practice good thoughts, good words, good deeds." Then the priest sprinkles the initiate with rose water. She is now bound forever to the "adoration of Ahura (the high God), renunciation of Satan, purity of soul, mind and body." From this time on she wears next to her body a white sacred shirt. This *navjote* ceremony is also a festive occasion, including feasting and many gifts. No child will ever forget such an occasion. (However Pervin, the Parsi neighbor girl of this ceremony, later learned to love the Lord Jesus Christ. When she was baptized she was disinherited because she broke the *navjote* vow. Her earthly family count her as dead; her only family is the family of God.)

Thirteen is counted as the important decision age among the Jewish people for boys and girls. According to their tradition a child of this age is old enough to understand the meaning and purpose of the commandments of the Jewish faith. Before this age he is expected to have a good knowledge of the Bible (Old Testament) and Jewish history and to be able to recite prayers in Hebrew. The special occasion for initiation is called *bar mitzvah* and is celebrated the first Sabbath after a boy's thirteenth birthday, usually in a synagogue. The high point of the ceremony is reached when the boy is called to the reading desk to chant benedictions before and after the Torah is read, and then to chant the selection from the Prophets. After this the boy is usually expected to address the congregation briefly. Following this service the parents are hosts to the festive part of the ceremony and again gifts are the order of the day. After this important day the lad has all the privileges of an adult member of the synagogue. He is responsible for his own behavior. From now on he will fast and pray as his father does and go with him to the synagogue.

We do not know what they did for the boy of this age in Jesus' day, but when He was twelve years old He went to the temple with His parents for the great Passover Feast. He had already developed great responsibility; His parents did not feel the need of keeping tab on Him. His sense of kinship with the heavenly Father was greater than His relationship to His earthly family, so He neglected to go home when they did. He was surprised at His parents' reproval when they returned to get Him, "Why were you searching for me? Didn't you know I had to be in my Father's house?" (Luke 2:41–52). This was not youthful rebellion on the part of the boy Jesus, because He returned with them to Nazareth "and was obedient to them."

Many young people do not have an encounter with the Lord because they do not know enough about Him. But if they do know about Him they will come to the time for decision. This seems to be true even when all other background is against such an experience. I shall never forget the story "Brother Leonard," a missionary in India, told me about his childhood in England. His parents were artists and they had both grown tired of being considered *different* because they were Jewish. They decided that their son should not have to go through life as they had, and so, when Leonard was eight they sent him to a Christian boarding school. They told the teachers that Leonard was to be treated and taught just like the boys from Christian families. He was not to think of himself as being different.

For the first time Leonard heard the stories of Jesus. Each day passages from the gospels were read in school without comment. It wasn't long until Jesus became his hero. He looked forward eagerly each day to the time for Scripture reading. When Leonard was thirteen the rest of his group entered a confirmation class. When the Jewish lad found out that this was preparation for becoming a disciple of Jesus he was delighted beyond measure! He hadn't realized before that such a thing was possible. But the headmaster of the school, fearing this was going too far, told Leonard they would have to get his parents' permission. The parents were stunned. They hadn't counted on anything like this, but they didn't want to spoil the fellowship their son had had in this school he loved so much. After serious consideration they decided he was *only* thirteen and he would surely soon forget this experience when he went on to other schools, so they gave their permission for Leonard to become a Christian.

The boy was delighted and he was a most studious and eager pupil as he learned what it meant to be a Christian. Then he was baptized and he took his first communion. Some twenty years later when he told me this story in India he added with great warmth: "Before that communion Jesus was my hero, but in some way I cannot yet explain, as I took communion, Jesus, my hero, became Jesus, my Savior. I knew His living presence. He holds me to this day.'' God *can* reach through to youth!

For a generation or more we have given young people freedom without commensurate responsibility, and we have been cynical about the idealism of youth. Instead of directing youth to the goal of Christian maturity we have told them not to trust their emotions, even the good ones. ''I felt that way when I was your age, but it passed with my youth,'' seems to be the theme song of many adults as they talk to young people. Their cynicism has undercut the very thing that should be happening to every young person. Many people are cynical because they did not keep on in the way they started. But that is no argument against starting; it is only an argument for learning *how to keep on* in God's way. Of one thing I am sure, we have far too long ignored early adolescence as an important time for reality in the things of the Spirit. When high school and college youth lay aside the ''faith of their childhood'' they are in reality merely laying aside their *childhood conceptions,* and their *credulity* even of good things, their security in imitating the ways of their own particular heritage. They are stretching out to new ideas that must be tested; they want to look over the walls that once protected them. They want to test the old ideas too, but they are too quickly criticized for even questioning them. They want a *faith* and not the credulity of childhood. It takes strong foundations and strong inner resources to ride through the pressures of thirteen to twenty. This strength comes through personal relationships, and above all through an experience of growing faith in Christ the Lord.

Exchanging the credulity of childhood (which is proper in childhood) for the maturing faith of adulthood is often a precarious transaction. If a child has only ideas *about* God he may not have enough experience to make the transaction. He may think he is leaving the credulity of childhood when he is merely changing what he is credulous about. He is drifting or rebelling when he ought to be *deciding.* For he has come to the place where he sees two ways of doing things. He sees the old familiar ways and the new unknown ways, and he cannot stand still. If he drifts, he will be a tool to be manipulated by anyone in his future; if he rebels, he will remain a helpless creature of his past. If he wants to be *somebody* he must be able to make a decision wisely.

The decision for Christ is the most important decision anyone can make. Anyone who is old enough to make a decision and who knows about Christ is old enough to make his decision for Him. It is the basic decision of life that will give discernment for all other decisions. Jesus is the *Way*, the *Truth*, the *Life* and the *Light* to reveal the right in any other decision. The decision means no to everything that is not Christlike and yes to everything that is His way and truth. The decision for Christ is more than a decision, it is a personal commitment of one's life to Him. The decision is our part in the new relationship to Him. He never decides for us, but He reaches out to us with all the love of God, waiting for us to decide for Him.

Facing the issue of this decision is often spoken of as an *encounter*. This means that it is more than making a decision about one's own life; it is making a decision for Someone and the decision must be followed by a commitment to Him for life. God does His part and then we do our part. The *new birth* becomes a fact. He comes to us, we come to Him, and then *by faith* we are born into the family of God as truly as we were first born into our earthly family.

When a baby is born his mother knows that the act of birth has been completed. But she also knows that this is not the whole story, for it is the beginning of a long, new story. The same thing is true when we are born into the family of God; we are now in the family, but we have to grow up. Many people forget about this growing up after they are born again. Because they forget about the growing up they think the new birth experience is the whole story. Some adults hold young people back until they are mature in other ways before they commit their lives to God, while others encourage very little children to come and they take the witness of a six-year-old as a completed experience. Premature babies have a hard time living, especially without proper care. The decision and the commitment to Him in any case, at any age, are just the beginnings of the new life.

This decision to become a member of the family of God includes joining the church but that is not all of it, as some children have been led to think. Some adults, even ministers, approach the young people and say, "You are old enough to join the church. Would you like to be in the pastor's class?" "If the rest of the kids do, I will," may be the casual answer to such a question. One large church in Chicago found that after the pastor's class training and acceptance into membership, the group quit coming to Sunday school. They thought they had graduated and they didn't come to church, either. They unfortunately missed getting any idea of a life purpose, a commitment to Christ, or any relevant meaning of church to their daily lives. They just felt "advanced." Their leaders tried so hard to avoid emotion in religion that they succeeded too well!

Many have been afraid of emotion because too many people have overemphasized the emotional part of such an experience. But the trouble is not with emotion; it is with *misused, uncontrolled, unguided emotion.* Emotion is a gift from God. Controlled emotion guided in proper channels is power. Knowing to do good is never enough. Emotional desire becomes the taproot of our ethics. Stirred emotion channeled into proper action means growth. Young people should never be chided for being emotional; they should be encouraged into the right action and they will need every bit of emotion that comes natural to them to follow through. A group of church district youth leaders reconsecrated their lives in a meeting one night. They were deeply moved. After the meeting four of the girls were huddled together in the back of the church, laughing and crying. The laughing and crying did not matter but their conversation did matter. To my surprise, they were not talking about how they *felt* in their new commitment to Christ but, very practically, they were discussing how they could live out this new commitment of life in their high school and in their social affairs. It will take all the emotion of their love for Christ to carry them through the pressures they have to face.

If the *experience* is held up as an end in itself many will lose their way. Edna was very happy after she decided to give her life to the Lord, but after she was immersed in baptism her happiness left her. She could not understand this because she expected her joy to increase. Her trouble was that she expected to have an experience in the water like her close friend had had. So while she was being baptized she was not thinking of her Savior, but she was looking in her heart to see an experience happen! No one ever had an *experience of Christ* by looking at himself. This is subtle temptation that sometimes comes when we hear the witness of another.

No two people are alike. We differ in our feelings about one another and in our feelings about God. *How we feel* is not the test of an experience of God. On the day of Pentecost, the disciples had the greatest experience of God that is possible to man, but they did not sit around comparing notes about how they felt. They were not even conscious of their own feelings: their consciousness was of the power of the Spirit. When the emphasis is on *Christ* rather than an *experience* of Him one need never fall into the mistaken idea that when he is too tired to have feelings about anything he has lost Christ. Our feelings never separate us from our Lord: only our unwillingness to do His will can separate us. Otherwise we live in the faith in His grace for the new relationship with Him.

So it is not the experience itself. All religions know how to contrive a religious experience, but a Christian experience is an experience of *Christ* through the Holy Spirit. When one has an experience of *Him* all else in life takes second place and everything must be pleasing to Him.

The *coming in* (Eph. 3:13–21), the *blessing,* the *guidance* and the *growing power* are God's part of the new relationship. Our part is to respond to His love and to accept His grace and by faith we become His children. We parents and teachers need to walk in reverence before Him if we want our children to know Him too. Let us think it through together again with Him: *At whatever age your child becomes interested in belonging to the Lord, the time is right.* And the step taken with the child's will be sealed by the tender Holy Spirit of Jesus Christ, whose love for that child surpasses any love we can comprehend. Your part as parents and teachers has helped prepare the young person for this step. His new Savior will be no stranger to him if you have nurtured his natural God hunger from his birth to this shining moment of his new birth.

Coming to God is not a foreign thing to a child. Adults knowingly or unknowingly block or clear his way. If you have been a way-clearer, his moment of encounter with God through Christ will be to the child the next normal, desirable step in the exciting business of growing up. If unconsciously you have put blocks in the child's way to God because of your own problems, His forgiveness waits for you, and, with your acceptance of His forgiveness, the blocks in your child's path will be pushed away. Jesus Christ is saying to all of us, "Let the children come to Me!"

Chapter 15

Responsibility of Grownups in God's Family

The story of the great encounter usually sounds like the stories ending with, "They were married, and lived happily ever after." Actually the report of the encounter is a birth announcement. Days of concern as well as joy lie ahead. Does the new baby take nourishment properly? Is he growing properly? Is he responding properly? These expectations are just as important after spiritual birth as after physical birth.

Those associated with a new Christian, especially one of tender age, are often unaware of the new sensitiveness to the Spirit of those just born into the kingdom. The following letter was published in a Christian paper in India. It was written by a thirteen-year-old boy to his mother and was shared with the son's permission:

> Dear Mother,
>   Since two months ago the Lord has helped me. On Sundays now the sermons make me determined to be good and to help others in the dorm. By Saturdays I'd practically lose my courage to help others but could defend myself from anything that is definitely wrong. Every night after lights are out, first I try to think of my own wrong doings, then in what places I could help others. I used to think that I committed only a few sins, maybe one in a few days, but now I understand that I have a long way to go.
>   After my conversion I was filled with the Holy Spirit all day. In the nights I'd cry over the many times I'd yielded to temptation. Then for a mere day I became a boy again disobeying and having a good time, and felt awfully unhappy after dark when I suddenly jumped as I understood my wrongdoings. Am spiritually happy now,
>
> Much love,
> Your son

The new sensitiveness to right and wrong is evident in this boy's letter. This sensitiveness is part of the new life but it needs to be guarded in order to keep it healthy. The tendency to try in one's own strength may linger and this will lead to discouragement. The greatest danger to the new Christian, especially one young in years, is self-condemnation because of this new sensitiveness. The acceptance of forgiveness at the time of conversion brings release from self-condemnation and fills one with joy. Many do not realize that this *forgiveness is continuous* every day, that one lives daily by the very grace through which redemption came in the first place.

The new insight, "Now I understand that I have a long way to go," should always be recognized as evidence of walking in the light. In the dark we cannot see the way. I wish someone had told me when I was a new Christian at the age of ten that the new ability to *see* mistakes more clearly was because I had new *light* and not that I was more in the wrong. It took me a long time to learn about continuous forgiveness and to know how to learn from my mistakes as I could now see them. In fact, that is why the Spirit reveals them to us: so that we can grow out of the old ways into His new ways. Help the new Christian to rejoice when he can see where he fails and help him to know what to do about it.

All older Christians also carry a special responsibility for showing the infinite patience and forgiveness of God toward the new babe in Christ. It is so easy for church women to discuss the "doings" and "goings on" of the young ones while they sit together sewing for the missionary needs. It is doubly hard for the youth to accept the forgiveness of God if their elders do not join the Lord in this act of love. This is the reason Jesus said it is so important not to cause one of these little ones to stumble (Matt. 18:1–6).

After the joys of the new experience in Christ many young Christians do not realize how much of the new life is one of *faith*. A new Christian told me she found this out to her surprise. She said she often felt like she was going through a fog, but she found if she did not get worried she always came out into the sunshine again. Others do not learn so quickly, especially if the *feeling* of the new experience has been overemphasized. Seemingly "low periods" are times for new lessons in faith. This faith is not in ourselves, or even in any past experience we have had, but it is *faith in the Lord* to whom we have given our lives. Of course, there is the possibility that the "fog" is a check of the Spirit for us to correct some mistake. If it is such a check of the Spirit He will always reveal that to us, so we still have no reason to worry. We can always trust His faithfulness.

The new adolescent Christian will have days of great emotional stress and turmoil, partly because of the ups and downs of growing from childhood to adulthood. An adult must be patient in helping him to sort out the real from the artificial, but he must also leave the youth enough freedom to think for himself, through the fog or the storm. It is much easier for an adult to give arbitrary answers, but these do not often help youth to find their own way; sometimes such answers only increase the conflict. The adult who can truly help the new Christian is the one who can help him quiet down and come into the Great Presence where one is always set free for clear thinking as well as for renewed relationship.

Other conflicts come because friends think in different ways. Some friends belong to other churches and are conscientious about doing things in a different way. Some friends may even be of a different faith. Sometimes it comes closer home than that, like the young girl who asked, ''My parents conscientiously believe one way, I conscientiously believe another. How can I get along with my parents?'' The difference of opinion of conscientious people often becomes bewildering, even to older Christians. Some young people hastily resolve the issue by saying, ''Oh, any way will do! Just so you believe it!'' But this is never the answer.

For one thing, the points on which different Christian churches agree are so much more important than the things on which they differ. We must always *go to center* and do our thinking from there about the beliefs nearer the periphery, even though these peripheral beliefs are important too.

The question of *mode* of baptism came up not long ago in a interdenominational youth group. Many were bewildered, but the Southern Baptists were sure of themselves and so were the Southern Methodists. The youth leaders in these two groups were good friends but quite argumentative. A Southern Baptist asked, ''Isn't it true that no one is really baptized unless he is dipped down under the water?'' Then he looked at his Methodist buddy with a teasing smile. The young man sitting next to me was one of the most honored spiritual leaders in the group. I asked the Baptist questioner, "Do you count this fellow beside me as a real Christian?" "Of course," he answered. Then I turned to the young man who was a Quaker, "They didn't use any water on you, did they?" He said, "No." Then I turned to the Methodist buddy and said, "They *sprinkled* you, didn't they?" "Yes." "And you don't remember anything about it, do you?" And he said, "No." One Mennonite was present, so I said to him, "They *poured* water on you, didn't they?" Then I came back to the Baptist questioner, "But they *dipped* you, didn't they?—down under the water?" With deep satisfaction he answered, "Yes, they did!" I added, "They dipped you once, didn't they?" "Yes," he answered, wondering what more there could be. Then I said, "Well, they dipped me *three times!*"

Laughter lifted the baptism question out of the field of argument. Then we got together on a discussion of the real meaning of baptism and entrance into a new life. No amount of water is of any value if the life is not changed. Paul said one's character is to be changed. As long as we emphasize the central meanings we are not so liable to get lost on difference in interpretation and method. Then we find we do not have to defy our own heritage, but we are free to follow our Lord in the footsteps of our fathers without stumbling over other interpretations. Our real unity is in Christ.

Adolescent years are school years. The new Christian may have teachers who do not know it is possible to have a relationship with God. He may even have teachers who unwisely taunt him for being "naive" in having faith in God. Youth need to be assured that we do not need to defend the truth of our faith. *We only witness to our faith in the truth.* A cynical person is challenged to dispute an argument, but it is difficult for him to tear down a *witness!*

Thinking years are questioning years. They may even be doubting years. The most important thing to ask of a young person is that he be *honest.* He needs to learn to think. He needs time to think. No older Christian should ever be shocked at any questions that sound like doubts, but should help every questioner keep close to the heavenly Father who understands questioning minds. Any honest person will be able to find the truth. This is the integrity Jesus asked of every follower.

As inquiring young people seek truth in the scientific world by scientific methods they need to be encouraged to continue with open, honest minds to read and receive the *revealed* Word of God. They must remember that there are two ways to truth. One is in man's own search. God does not reveal to man what he can find out for himself. No one can neglect the study of his algebra and then expect God to reveal the answers to him on examination day. But there are other truths man cannot find out by his own research. These are revealed by the illumination of the Holy Spirit. One must respond to the love of God as revealed in Jesus Christ in order to be able to know this revealed truth. No one can expect a vision from heaven to tell him the truths already revealed in God's Word. This is the reason it is so important to know God's Word. A family that has been faithful together in Bible reading and prayer will be a great asset to any new Christian in his own private discipline and discernments.

While still so inexperienced, young people face the three greatest decisions of life. The first, *for God;* we hope they settle this first. The next one that must be considered seriously is that of *vocation.* Jesus said we could depend on the Holy Spirit to guide us (John 16:13). Sometimes when young people do look to God for guidance the result is hard for the parents to take. The parents may offer opinions and counsel, but the decision lies with the young person and his Lord. The parents must learn to take this. A consecrated girl offered herself for foreign service, putting God's call above the desire of her parents. Her devout aunt wrote to the parents, "The news was like a bolt from the blue and I can imagine how it must have rocked your world. She is such a dedicated girl, however, and so completely honest, that any decision she makes deserves the respect and backing of us all. But we'll miss her." This is the attitude the grownups in the family of God should take to the younger ones in the family.

The third great decision, often made before the teen years are gone, is that of a *life companion.* But whether this decision is made early or late the social life as well as the spiritual life of the teen years will be deciding factors in *preparation* for marriage. Many young people have said, "It's easy to be a Christian at church, my problem is how to be a Christian on a date." Surely it is not "Victorian" but Christian to say that a person should feel just as clean after a date as after a

communion service. Older people fail the young people so often by their teasing or unsympathetic remarks. *Only loving understanding helps.*

The church must be interested in the social life of its young people because it is interested in the young people. Anything "social" that the church sponsors for the young people should never be planned to compete with the secular entertainment field. The church is not in the entertainment business. But *because* young people are social beings, in training (whether they know it or not) for all future human relationships, the church should help to care for the whole of their lives.

Those stormy times come to young people too, when there is nothing an adult can do for them but to stand by and wait to be needed. Any adult who loves a young person and finds himself in this place of waiting to be needed will find that he is not alone in the waiting line. The heavenly Father has been there all the time waiting for us all to know how much we need Him. When we really wait with and on the "Waiting Father," the door opens for the miracle of God's love to work in some way for our loved ones.

This "miracle" happened to a dear friend of mine and her daughter Sally. But first I must introduce Sally as I met her. She was eight years old then and had come with her mother from a southern city to a summer conference in the far north. Before they left home, and all the way on the train, the mother could not find words to explain to Sally that blacks would be in this conference right along with the white people so she didn't try. The third evening of the conference came and still no word had been said. But as Sally sat on the edge of the bed taking off her shoes, all of a sudden she said, "Mother, do you know what?" Her mother thought, "Now this is it!" Then Sally blurted out, "We are up here in a mess of Yankees!"

Sally was a loved and a disciplined girl. She was both obedient and self-assertive. Her obedience was a natural consequence of her home-life. Her self-assertion reflected her parents' willingness for her to grow in her own way and to make her own decisions, and her remark surely reflected Sally's eagerness to do both under her own steam. In high school Sally, in the much coveted role of "cheerleader," and the star football player became "steadies." They had nothing in common but football and youth. Some days her mother could not help but perceive evidences of cruelty on her daughter. Then Sally would have days of depression from the boy's possessiveness and an estrangement at home because of her misery. She was sinking in the sands of emotional immaturity. Her parents saw her future threatened, but were helpless to do anything but wait and pray.

With fear and determination one day Sally announced her coming wedding. Then quite unexpectedly, on top of her concern for her daughter, Sally's mother found herself with a girl on her hands—a runaway girl whom the town sheriff asked her to befriend. To get away from her mother this unloved girl was going to marry a fellow who would take her if no one else would.

The two girls were together in Sally's room, two girls planning runaway weddings that very day! While Sally talked the sense she really had to this other girl and persuaded her to return to her mother and not make a foolish marriage, she herself became free from her own obsession of several years. Sally's mother knows now that when she forgot her own heartache to save another girl from an unwise marriage, God intervened to save her own daughter! (The runaway girl has since married a Baptist minister and Sally a beloved doctor. Both are happy and free.)

In giving permission to use this story Sally's mother added: "This is a success story. But not every girl escapes an unwise marriage, and not all parents who pray and wait are favored with the miracle we had. Parents are those people who wait. They wait and have faith in the good seeds they've sown, but often there is a crop failure. Then what? Our children make their mistakes; God gives us strength to suffer with them. There are regrets, but there need be no bitterness. That also is God's gift!"

Keeping our hearts open to the heavenly Father so He can work through us is our greatest responsibility to Him and to our loved ones. Four-year-old Becky was walking in the woods in the early spring with her mother. They were enjoying the beautiful blossoms along the way that God had created. When they came into the house Becky stood in front of the French windows, closed because the air was still chilly, and called to her mother, "Let's open the windows and let God come in here, too.'' Becky did not know yet that God cannot be penned out by closed windows, only by closed hearts.

Parents and teachers with closed hearts (even if they have ''correct doctrine'') can be responsible for closing the hearts of children and young people brought into their care. God Himself, in Jesus Christ, demonstrated His *open heart* on His cross. No adult can ever hope to force or even push a child into the kingdom of God. But any adult can allow the loving Spirit of the Father to move through his or her available and open heart, toward the hearts of the little ones He loves so much. Since He never forces His way into any heart He waits for those of us older in the family of God to represent Him truly to the younger ones. He still stands at the door and knocks saying, ''If anyone hears My voice and opens the door, I will come in and eat with him, and he with me'' (Rev. 3:20).

Bibliography

Ansuble, David Paul, M.D., Ph.D., *Theory and Problems of Child Development*, Grimes and Stratton, New York, 1958.

Arbaugh, George B., *Growth of a Christian*, Muhlenberg Press, Philadelphia, 1953.

Arnold, Arnold, *How to Play With Your Child*, Ballantine Books, No. 105.

Barrett, T. Van B., *The Christian Family*, Morehouse-Gorham, 1958.

Baruch, Dorothy W., *New Ways in Discipline*, McGraw-Hill Book Co., 1949.

Benson, C. B., *A Popular History of Christian Education*, Moody Press, Chicago, 1943.

Black, Irma Simonton, *Off to a Good Start*, Harcourt, Brace & Co., 1953.

Caldwell, Irene Smith, *Our Concern Is Children*, Warner Press, Anderson, Indiana, 1948.

————, *Teaching That Makes a Difference*, Warner Press, Anderson, Indiana, 1950.

Campbell, Elizabeth W., *Security for Young Children*, Pilgrim Press, 1952.

Camper, Mrs. Shirley, *How to Get Along With Your Child*, Belmont Books, New York, 1962.

Carson, Fred Pierce, *The Christian Imprint*, Abingdon, 1955.

Chamberlain, John Gordon, *Parents and Religion*, Westminster, 1961.

Cully, Iris V., *Children in the Church*, Westminster, 1960.

Edge, Findlay B., *Teaching for Results*, Broadman Press, Nashville, Tenn., 1956.

Erb, Alta Mae, *Christian Nurture of Children*, Herald Press, Scottdale, Penna., 1955.

Fritz, Dorothy B., *The Spiritual Growth of Children*, Westminster, 1957.

Gebhard, Edward W. and Anna Laura, *Guideposts to Creative Family Worship*, Abingdon, 1953.

Hamilton, Mrs. Clarence H., *Our Children and God*, Bobbs-Merrill Co., 1952.

Heron, Frances Dunlap, *Kathy Ann, Kindergartner*, Abingdon, 1955.

Jaarsma, Cornelius, *Fundamentals in Christian Education*, William B. Eerdmans Publishing Co., 1953.

Jones, Mary Alice, *Guiding Our Children in Christian Growth*, Abingdon, 1949. (and other books)

Kawin, Ethel, *The Wise Choice of Toys*, University of Chicago Press, 1934.

Keplar, Hazel, *The Child and His Play*, Funk and Wagnalls, 1952.

Loomis, Earl A. J., M.D., *The Self in Pilgrimage*, Harpers. 1960.

Maynard, Donald M., *Your Home Can Be Christian*, Abingdon, 1952.

Menninger, Wm. C., M.D., *How You Grow Up*, Sterling Publishing Co. Inc., New York, 1957.

Miller, Randolph Crump, *Education for Christian Living*, Prentice-Hall Inc., 1956.

————, *Your Child's Religion*, Doubleday & Co. Inc., 1962.

Price, Eugenia, *Beloved World*, Zondervan, 1962.

————, *Find Out for Yourself*, Zondervan, 1963.

Rasey, Marie L. and Menge, J. W., *What We Learn From Children*, Harpers, 1956.

Reed, William W., *Teaching the Church's Children*, Morehouse-Gorham, 1958.

Reeves, Katherine, *Children, Their Ways and Wants*, Educational Publishing Corp., Darien, Conn., 1959.

Roberts, Guy L., *How the Church Can Help Where Delinquency Begins*, John Knox Press, 1958.

Robertson, Josephine, *How to Help Through Understanding*, Abingdon, 1961.

Royal, Claudia, *Teaching Your Child About God*, Revell, 1960.

Sherrill, Lewis J., *The Opening Doors of Childhood*, Macmillan, 1950.

————, *The Struggle of the Soul*, Macmillan, 1952.

————, *The Gift of Power*, Macmillan, 1955.

Smart, James D., *The Teaching Ministry of the Church*, Westminster, 1954.

Steere, Douglas V., *On Listening to Another*, Harpers, 1955.

Trent, Robbie, *Your Child and God*, Willit, Clarke & Co., 1941.

Vandervelde, Frances, *Christian Home and Family Living*, Zondervan, 1959.

Webb, Lance, *Discovering Love*, Abingdon, 1959.

Whitehouse, Elizabeth S., *The Children We Teach*, Judson, 1950.

Whyte, Dorothy K., *Teaching Your Child Right From Wrong*, Bobbs-Merrill, 1961.

Williams, John G., *Worship and the Modern Child*, Macmillan, 1958.

Williams, Norman V., *The Christian Home*, Moody, 1952.

Wittenberg, Rudolph M., *Adolescence and Discipline*, Association Press, 1959.

Wycoff, D. Campbell, *The Task of Christian Education*, Westminster, 1959.

————, *The Gospel and Christian Education*, Westminster, 1959.

Wynn, J. C., *How Parents Face Family Problems*, Westminster, 1954.

Yoder, Gideon G., *The Nurture and Evangelism of Children*, Herald Press, Scottdale, Penna., 1959.

Sources for Helpful Pamphlets. Catalogues available.

American Medical Association, 535 N. Dearborn St., Chicago 10, Ill.

Association for Family Living, 32 W. Randolph St., Chicago 1, Ill.

Child Study Association of America, Inc., 9. E. 89th St., New York 28.

Child Welfare League of America, Inc., 44 E. 23rd St., New York 10.
Children's Bureau, U. S. Depart. of Health, Education and Welfare, Washington 25, D. C.
Family Service Association of America, 215 Park Ave., S., New York 3.
National Congress of Parents and Teachers, 700 N. Rush St., Chicago 11, Ill.
Public Affairs Committee, Inc., 22 E. 38th St., New York 16.
Science Research Associates, Inc., 259 E. Erie St., Chicago 11, Ill.
Your Own Church Publishing House.